The *SECRET* LIFE *of* MEN

The *SECRET* LIFE *of* MEN

A Practical Guide to Helping Men
Discover Health, Happiness and
Deeper Personal Relationships

STEVE BIDDULPH

MARLOWE & COMPANY
NEW YORK

THE SECRET LIFE OF MEN: *A Practical Guide to Helping Men Discover Health, Happiness and Deeper Personal Relationships*

Copyright © Steve and Shaaron Biddulph 1994, 1995, 2003

Published by
Marlowe & Company
An Imprint of Avalon Publishing Group Incorporated
161 William Street, 16th Floor
New York, NY 10038

Originally published in Australia and New Zealand as *Manhood: An Action Plan for Changing Men's Lives* by Finch Publishing Pty Limited, Sydney.

Library of Congress Cataloging-in-Publication Data
Biddulph, Steve.
  [Manhood]
  The secret life of men : a practical guide to helping men discover health, happiness, and deeper personal relationships / Steve Biddulph.
    p. cm.
  Previous published as: Manhood, 1998.
  Includes bibliographical references and index.
  ISBN 1-56924-481-2 (pbk.)
    1. Men–Psychology. 2. Men–Family relationships. 3. Masculinity. 4. Sex role.
  5. Men's movement. I. Title.

  HQ1090.B52 2003
  305.31–dc21

                                                                    2002045520

ISBN 1-56924-494-4

9 8 7 6 5 4 3 2 1

Designed by Simon M. Sullivan
Printed in the United States of America
Distributed by Publishers Group West

C O N T E N T S

The SECRET LIFE of MEN

1 **The Problem**

MOST MEN DON'T have a life. Instead we have an act, an outer show, kept up for protection. We pretend things are fine, that everything is cool, and sometimes we even fool ourselves. But ask a man how he really feels or what he really thinks, and the first thing he thinks is "What am I supposed to say?" The average man today is deeply unhappy, but he would be the last to admit it.

Most women are not like this. Women today act from inner feeling and spirit, and more and more they know who they are and what they want. The Women's Movement helped this along, but women were always more in touch with themselves and each other. The men in relationships with these strong and healthy women are no match for them, in every sense of that word. Conversations go nowhere, and relationships collapse, because to be in a relationship, you have first to know who you are, and the man does not have this worked out.

How did this come about? Put in very simplified terms, boys growing up over the last few generations did not learn how to be men, because no one ever taught them or showed them how. Our culture forgot how to do this. In the twentieth century, men almost disappeared from the lives of children. Communities disintegrated, and men withdrew from each other. Work became our only purpose. And so the software of healthy maleness was essentially lost. While our ideas of how to be a woman blossomed and deepened and enriched themselves in the twentieth century, our ideas of how to be a man went backwards.

If you have watched children grow up, you will have seen this tragedy unfold. Little children of both sexes start out well enough; they are alive to themselves, expecting to be joyful, expecting life to be an adventure. But early on, a boy's spirit begins to shrivel. Something essential is not being provided. By the time he is a man, he is like a tiger raised in a zoo—confused and numb, with huge energies untapped. He feels that there must be more to life, but he does not know what that "more" is. So he spends his life pretending—to his friends, his family, and himself—that everything is okay, and hoping that something, somehow, might happen to make this come true.

CRACKS IN THE FACADE

Pretending all the time is very hard work, and so it's not surprising that cracks often start to appear in a man's façade. Sometimes this can happen in a positive way. A man may chance upon a taste of what things could be like—a fleeting glimpse of being fully alive. Perhaps he is alone on a beach or a mountaintop, and suddenly the glory of the physical world breaks in on him, he feels himself dissolved in the wind and sky. Or he is playing with his children, and suddenly he is a child again himself, tingling with life. Sometimes a passage of music can do it. Or it can come in certain kinds of moments with a woman—passion, tenderness, or simple compassion melts through his defenses. He glimpses something magical . . . but then it is gone. He almost feels worse for the experience, bereft, not knowing how to recapture that feeling. So he shuts the memory away, and gets on with "business as usual."

Often though, the cracks happen in more painful ways—through relationship breakdown, business setbacks, injury, or a terrible accident. The thing that keeps him going—the dream of one day arriving at the happiness or peace he seeks, suddenly is snatched away. A deep despair settles on him as he realizes that those closest to him not only do not *love* him, they do not even *know* him. His connection to his own life suddenly appears to be the thinnest of threads, ready to break at any moment.

Some months back, I met with a group of school principals on a Monday morning. They were very quiet, and when I asked why, they told me that one of their colleagues, a man in his late thirties, had just that weekend taken his own life. Rejected by his wife, humiliated that her affair with another man had become public knowledge, he had put on diving weights and leapt into the sea and drowned.

In my final year of high school, a good friend who had consistently had the highest grades all through school, only received five honors instead of the six he had hoped for in the final exams. He waited till his brother, who shared his bedroom, had fallen asleep, and then taking a gun he had hidden under the bed, he walked silently out onto the river bank behind his home and ended his life.

Both of these were good and caring men. They had a network of people around them who would have done anything they could to help. The problem was the armor we have around us. Because the man feels he cannot voice the problem, that he is not supposed to *have* a problem, the help and love is untapped. A man dies, or he goes on suffering alone, in the mistaken belief that no one cares. (Many movies have explored this—from Robert Redford's classic *Ordinary People*, to the more recent *My Life as a House*. It's a central theme of our culture, and will be until we solve it.)

Several years ago in the city where I lived, a young man went to see a lingerie fashion show in a large department store. The event featured the supermodel Elle McPherson, whose line of raunchy underwear was being "launched." No one knows what went on in the young man's mind. Perhaps he struggled to resolve the feelings of shame and arousal that swirled through his body. Perhaps he was angered by the erotic posturing of women who would certainly offer him no love. Whatever it was, he suddenly he climbed onto the stage, and shouted "You whore!" into the face of the supermodel. Cameras flashed—newspapers the next day showed his face—it was pure rage. He was quickly dragged away by security guards. He ran straight to a tall building nearby, went up to the roof, and leapt to his death. Certainly he was a disturbed young man. But that doesn't mean he didn't have something to say.

In each of these situations and in all the male tragedies you ever heard of in your own neighborhood, town, or city, there is a common thread. An unbearable tension between the human needs of a man and the role he is supposed to play. What we are asking of men might be impossible.

The evidence makes it clear (see the box on next page) that all through the last century, and into this one, men have been suffering disproportionately. Not just through suicide, but premature death from stress and neglect of one's own health, motor vehicle and workplace accidents, and alcohol and drug addiction. These statistics are all dominated by men. And men who are hurting also tend to hurt others. Physical violence against spouses, sexual abuse, schoolyard shootings, divorce, moral bankruptcy in business and politics, and certainly the sad state of world politics—all point to something seriously amiss with men.

That's as negative as we are going to get—we just hit bottom. This is a book about "Where to from here?" But first we have to grasp the scope of the problem. Everyone knows there are dysfunctional men—from the Washington Sniper right through to George Bush or Bill Clinton. But what we are proposing here is that these are not exceptions. These are the rule. Healthy men are a rarity. Something big, as big as feminism, as big as the civil rights movement, has to happen to help men change, to be freer, more open, more connected, and more whole.

How do we redeem and restore the health and happiness of men? How do we raise boys to be balanced, loving, and life-filled? That's what this book sets out to explore.

Facing the facts

- American men, on average, live for five years less than women do.
- American men have twice as many vehicle accidents, twice as many deaths from heart attacks, three times as many deaths from injuries, twice the deaths from liver disease. In fact, men exceed women in all thirteen leading causes of death.
- American men commit suicide at five times the rate of women.
- American men routinely fail at close relationships. (Just two indicators: around 50 percent of marriages break down, and two out of three divorces are initiated by the woman.)
- Over 90 percent of convicted acts of violence will be carried out by men, and 70 percent of the victims will be men.
- In school, around 90 percent of children with behavior problems are boys and over 80 percent of children with learning problems are also boys.
- Men comprise over 90 percent of the inmates in the prison system.

As Robert Bly once said—are you depressed enough already?

IN A NUTSHELL

• Most men are unhappy, most of the time.

• We learn early in life to pretend that things are fine.

• As a result, we live a pretend life, and those around us don't know us.

• Men have largely disappeared from the lives of children, and so boys can't learn healthy manhood.

• We are so used to dysfunctional men in politics, business, and the family, we don't realize how much happier and life-giving men could be, given the chance.

2 What Went Wrong?

DURING THE 1990S, writers and researchers around the world began pointing out something that should have been blindingly obvious, but had somehow gone unnoticed. This was that for hundreds of thousands of years of human history and pre-history, boys and girls did their growing up in the presence of men who cared about them actively, all day, every day. Then in the historical blink of an eye, with the coming of the industrial era and the death of villages, men began to disappear from the lives of children. Because of this, we are now living in the most under-fathered generation in human history.

Today, girls do not grow up in the company of many safe, healthy men, and so do not experience themselves other than as sex-objects—which the advertising media is quick to exploit. And boys are not given either the teaching, or the example, of how to be male, how to live in a male body with its unique hormonal patterns and responses and moods, in a healthy and constructive, socially integrated way.

With no deep training in masculinity, a boy's body will still turn into a man's body, that much is guaranteed. *But he will not be given the software.* Nobody passes on to him the inner knowledge and skills to match his powers or his yearnings. His father may wish to do so, may feel some dimly perceived impetus to give something in the way of wisdom or guidance, but he too lacks this, as did his own father before him. The most he can offer is a kind of friendship, which is not the same thing. So something biologically expected and needed does not occur, and development stalls.

Women are still closely involved in the care of children (though this too is being reduced by the pressures of the corporate world and how it would have us all live). Women, in a sense, have been left to hold it all together, and they do an extraordinary job. A boy's mother, and the other women in his life—school teachers and cub leaders, can give him much training in how to be *human*, but each of us is not just human, we are also male or female. And each of us needs help to deal with that extra burden, and extra potentiality. Older cultures provided this training intensively, the anthropology texts are full of the ways young people were trained into responsible and safe adulthood. But our culture is just too busy making money to be able to do it. For almost five generations now, the father-child link has been weakened. The time fathers spend with children actually interacting, laughing, talking, playing, teaching can be counted in minutes a day, at best. (In Japan it's even worse—most young children only see their fathers on weekends). And of course, many children do not have or see a father at all.

To make matters worse, those men who are around, and do care, have a lot to deal with. In the five generations since we left the villages for the cities with their factories and mills— five major wars have taken place, several deep recessions, migrations, relocations—all have added to the damage done to the male psyche. Many of the men who raised us were damaged, emotionally shut down, crushed by what they had seen and experienced.

The uncles and mentors of an earlier age have largely disappeared from the scene. Unless a boy is very talented at sport, is in the Boy Scouts, or encounters a very special schoolteacher, he may not come to know any good men closely at all. Not knowing the inner world of real men, each boy has to base his idea of self on a thinly drawn image gleaned from TV, the movies, and his peers—which he cobbles together into his male act. Jerry Seinfeld, Kurt Cobain, Arnold Schwarzenegger, Brad Pitt, mix and match, and take your pick. Each boy does his best to live his life using this one-dimensional façade, which is awfully hard to stretch around any of life's big challenges.

Girls, on the other hand, have a vastly different experience of growing up. From babyhood onward they receive a continuous exposure to competent and communicative women at home, at school, and later in their own friendship networks. From this they learn an open and sharing style of womanhood that enables them to get close to other women and give and receive support throughout their lives. Men's and boys' friendship networks—if they have them at all—are awkward and oblique, lacking in intimacy and often short term. (When my school days ended, I simply never saw my classmates again. Likewise when I left my university, and again with my first job. Today this appalls me, and I feel an aching wish to see those men and know how their lives have worked out.)

The lack of in-depth elder male connections during our childhoods leaves men bereft and struggling. Whether we are attempting to be "Sensitive New Men" or are clinging to the John Wayne, tough-guy image, we keep finding that it just doesn't work. The results are disastrous. Our marriages fail, our kids hate us, we die from stress, and on the way we destroy the world.

TROUBLE AT THE I'M OK, YOU'RE OK CORRAL

KNOWING WHERE TO BEGIN

If there is to be a first step in the healing of men, then it is probably to begin to be more truthful. Admitting that you are far from happy breaks the mold of denial and pretense.

It's no wonder we have a tradition of denial—for it served us well in the past. Men who are alive today are products of the most devastating century in history. Remember the opening scenes of *Saving Private Ryan*? The beaches of Normandy on D-Day, or any of the battlefields of World War II, Korea, Vietnam, or the Gulf War, were not places to get in touch with your feelings. (The Gulf War was where the Oklahoma bomber acquired his hatred of his country.) The Great Depression was no place to be giving in to sadness or fear. These were times for toughing it out. Author Mary Pipher, in her wonderful book *The Shelter of Each Other*, points out that America was virtually built on self-denial, because wallowing in feelings would have drowned us in despair. Self denial is an admirable survival skill, in the short term. But in the twentieth century, so much happened in such a short time, psychologically speaking, that it became a way of life.

Men became like logs of wood, shut down, unreachable, explosive.

Today men are starting to change, and the change begins with being emotionally honest. This doesn't mean weakness. A rhythm of strength and weakness, like a great tree swaying, is the secret of enduring. Let me illustrate what I mean. A friend of mine is a fire chief. Several years ago, he was the last one to leave the scene of a housefire in which two children had been burned to death. He secured the site, prepared to leave, but as he was leaving, he saw a melted toy duck on the back lawn of the burned-down house. His kids had a duck like that. He felt tears well up, and clung to a fence post for several minutes, sobbing. Then he went home, talked a little to his wife about it, and was fine. Another older fireman I knew never gave into his emotions, it was his proudest boast that he could handle anything in the line of duty. But he was in fact, away from the job, a tense man, who would explode suddenly and for the smallest of reasons. One day his wife told me he had smashed his daughter's stereo to pieces because she had too many appliances plugged into the wall outlet of her room. His kids hated him being around, they couldn't relax. Emotions don't go away when we deny them to ourselves, they just make us more dangerous.

One day each man has to stop running and take stock, and allow the truth of how his life is really going to come to the surface. Sometimes it takes a crisis of some kind to force this to happen. Whatever prompts the moment, as a man starts to really feel what he has lost in his life, the missed opportunities, the loneliness, he breaks through the numbness into a sharp and painful grief. This is a positive step, though it almost always feels worse. Change starts with acknowledging where you are—so important for us men—precisely because the denial of the pain is at the very core of what holds us in our inner prison. Grief is what happens as we start to become alive again after a period of deadening. Grief is a very subtle and wise emotion. It serves as both a renewal and a compass, since it involves surrendering, giving up the struggle, so that we can find our natural level of being; then as we do this, it starts us yearning for what we have lost. Only then, with our feet on solid ground for the first time, can we begin the journey to recover it. When we surrender, we become open to closeness, trust, friendship, creativity. Grief can be so much more fruitful than anger, which is a man's habitual reaction and one that has often been so destructive in our lives.

> Grief . . . starts us yearning for what we have lost, so we can begin the journey to recover it

A PICTURE OF HOPE

Women in the twentieth century had to overcome centuries of restriction and limitation on who they could be and what they could do, and so anger was the main emotion driving the women's movement. But men's difficulties are with isolation. The enemies, the prisons from which men have to escape, are:

- loneliness
- compulsive competition
- lifelong emotional timidity

Women's enemies were largely in the world around them. Men's enemies are out there too—in the pressure to work and earn and perform, but they are also very much on the inside—in the walls we put up around our own hearts.

Coming out from behind these walls (slowly, carefully) will allow dramatic and significant change. It will mean that men become more physically alive, sensing more, laughing more, responding more in body and mind—to our own benefit and to the great benefit of women and children. We will change jobs, change houses, take journeys, invest in our families and friends, join activist movements, dance and love more intensely. We will be safer and more woven into the fabric of life.

There is a lot of reason to be optimistic about this. Judging by the excitement, hope, and relief I encounter on radio talk shows, at public lectures, and on visits to different countries, many people are excited about this new way of looking at men's potentialities. Apart from the warmth and appreciation that men show for these ideas, there are other encouragements. After lectures, mothers of teenage sons come up to me with tears in their eyes, anxious and happy that something might really happen to improve their boys' self-esteem. Wives drag their husbands along. Single women, looking for a "real man" to relate to, urge me to "get on with it!"

Men are a problem to women, but rarely is this intentional. They are to an even greater degree a problem to themselves. The gender debate raged for thirty years, often fruitlessly, before we woke up to the fact that men are not winners, and never really were. Men and women are co-victims in a pattern of living and relating that is in drastic need of revision. Simply blaming men doesn't change a thing. We need help to change ourselves. Many people now are beginning to rethink what it means to be a man. Our choices of how to be a man were so limited. The suburban car polisher, the corporate drone, the sexually incompetent beer drinker with his baseball cap and his SUV—some choice!

What follows is a practical book about what you, as a man, can do to break out of the mold, and make a life that is authentic and free. And if you are a woman, about how you can help the men you care about to make these changes. The book cites some of the best ideas about masculine change, draws on many personal experiences, and is strongly flavored by the lives of men I have worked with around the world. It is written for older men, young men, working men, unemployed men, businessmen, farmers, fathers, sons, gay men, married men, black, white, and brown men; and, of course, for the women who love them and want to understand them and see them thrive.

IN A NUTSHELL

- The beginning of healing is to grieve for what you've lost.

- Men have three enemies—isolation from each other, bottling up emotions, and compulsive competition.

- These keep us apart, and keep us from getting the support we need.

- It's time to envisage, and become, a new kind of man.

OTHER VOICES

The mass of men lead lives of quiet desperation.

—Henry Thoreau, in *Walden*

Who taught us to be a man? Nobody!

—Marvin Allen

We are living at an important and fruitful moment now, for it is clear to men that the images of adult manhood given by popular culture are worn out; a man can no longer depend on them. By the time a man is thirty-five, he knows that the images of the right man, the tough man, the true man, which he received in high school, do not work in life. Such a man is open to new visions of what a man is or could be.

—Robert Bly in *Iron John*

Each man seems to be struggling with it quietly—at twenty-five, or thirty-five . . . men are at the edge of a momentous change in their very identity as men, going beyond the change catalyzed by the women's movement. It is a deceptively quiet movement, a shifting in direction, a saying "no" to old patterns, a searching for new values, a struggling with basic questions that each man seems to be dealing with alone.

—Betty Friedan in *The Second Stage*

Make no mistake about it: women want a men's movement. We are literally dying for it. . . . We have to use our instincts when deciding what to trust. We need to ask questions. . . . Then women can find allies in this struggle for a future that has never been.

—Gloria Steinem in
Women Respond to the Men's Movement

3 **Seven Steps to Manhood**

LET'S START WITH a simple question to you, as a man. Are you happy? Or are you just pretending to be and hoping that pretending will one day make it true? Do not answer this too quickly.

If the answer is no, then don't panic, and don't blame yourself for somehow having failed. There are reasons why this is true for most men, and there is a clear path forward that you can take to make your life very different.

The conditions under which we now raise human beings are so far from what is ideal, or even minimally necessary, that we are in need of a huge re-evaluation and a new way of organizing our lives and our choices. You personally can be part of this, ours is the turn-around generation that looked at our map and said—Wrong Way. Your own progress and healthy growth is needed to help others to follow. Your children and your friends and the women you care about will all benefit hugely from your investment in changing yourself along the lines that this book is about to uncover.

MENDING THE BROKEN CHAIN

Left alone, a seedling will grow into a tree and a tadpole will turn into a frog. But a human child does not turn into a functioning adult without lots of help. To learn to be the gender you are, you probably need thousands of hours of interaction with older, more mentally equipped members of your own gender.

Imagine if a little girl was born, and her mother died in childbirth. That she was raised by her single father, and for some reason her father lived in a place where there were very few women. All through her childhood and teenage years, she had no women to talk to, and her teachers at school and other caregivers were also all male. This little girl would probably grow to be healthy enough physically, but we would have real concerns for her development into a woman. We would see a real need for her to get some mothering, some time and help from aunts, women role models to help her understand life. We would be pretty alarmed. Yet this same-sex deprivation is the normal experience of millions of boys, and we don't even blink.

In our society, girls get deep contact from women on a day-to-day basis, but boys rarely get it from men. Women raise girls and boys, and most elementary school teachers are female. Most of the day, most of the time, men are usually not around in the lives of children. The result of this lack of male contact is a problem we are all aware of: in today's world, most little boys just grow into emotional children in adult bodies. The loneliness of this and the confusion—not knowing how to be comfortable with normal masculine feelings or how to be close to other males—cannot be understated, yet for most men it is so normal they do not even realize that it could be different.

DEVELOPING INTO A MAN

For boys and for adult men, for girls too, we have to rebuild a community of involved and healthy men, and we have to reconstruct the character and style of maleness. This is not to say there is any one model of how to be male. The more choices, examples, and varieties of maleness available, the better chance a boy has to say—"that man is like me," "that is the kind of man I want to become." In the same way a plant pulls out of the forest floor the ingredients it needs, a boy can choose and combine the nutrients that will complete him— the values, attitudes, information, physical behaviors, skills, and attributes that will work in the world we live in.

A male body has hormonal reactions, energies, neurological patterns, ways of perceiving, and ways of processing information that are male in style. There is wide variety, but there still is something called maleness. How to turn this into healthy maleness requires exposure to those who have solved the problems (for example) of being physically stronger than most women, of being somewhat less able with words than most women, of being powerfully and sometimes inappropriately attracted to women, and all the dilemmas that go with being male. How to deal with the cultural expectation to be a provider, to always be strong, the way the society wants to use you as factory or war fodder, or preys on your needs to make you buy things you don't need. Young men need older men to help with these things, and middle-aged men still need even older men, because each life stage is different and needs new information. If this need is met then life becomes vastly more bearable, secure, interesting, and friendly. The sense of lonely struggle and imminent failure is replaced with an experience of life as a supported journey to mastery.

Looking at this personally for a moment, if your developmental needs were not met in childhood and adolescence, you wouldn't necessarily know this. (Even children growing up in the most bizarre families assume that their life is normal.) You will only get a suspicion that things are amiss when your life starts to go wrong. This is what is happening to men today. Problems with health, marriage, parenthood, ability to make friends, and failure at work are some of the ways they are alerted to the deep holes in their being. As young men, we put on a cocky and cheerful face, but as the pressures of life stack up, our deficiencies become more obvious. The abysmal performance of our male leaders at all levels of society is a symptom of this problem. A male leader needs to draw on exceptional fathering experiences since he is father to a team, an organization, or even a country. The difference between Nelson Mandela and George Bush lies essentially in the kind of fathering they received. (Good women are needed too, to make a great man, but a good father or substitute father is the catalyst, the missing piece needed to meld it all together.)

> As young men we act cocky and cheerful, but as the pressures of life stack up, our deficiencies become more obvious

In nature, all development follows a laid-down sequence. In a man's development, the sequence has been forgotten and the process largely left to chance.

Over the last ten years, researchers and practitioners in the field of men's health and well-being have identified about seven key missing steps in men's development. These could be called the seven roads, or seven steps to manhood. The aim of these steps is not just to become well adjusted, i.e. shoe-horned to fitting into our rather toxic society. Nor are they solely about "personal development" or new age individualism. Like the women's movement, or civil rights, these changes will need the large world to change as well, and we will have to link up with many others to bring these things about. The aim is to win back control of our own lives, but this is inextricably tied up with reshaping the culture we live in—so that it is more life-affirming and less enslaving of men. Without idealizing things, it's possible to note that men have been at times in history much more exuberant and free, life-giving, creative, and whole. The Sioux hunter, the Masai warrior, the Aboriginal elder, and the medieval craftsman lived glorious and multi-dimensional lives—creative, sensual, spirited, and integrated around the care and protection both of their people and of the natural world. Why should today's man have to be any less a man than his ancestors?

SEVEN STEPS TO MANHOOD

The "steps" to full development as a man are clear and specific. They are not always easy or quick, but they offer a blueprint that is an enormous improvement over just getting through. To excite and provoke your interest, let's give a brief glimpse of the seven. Reading them in this way may just touch a chord in you that gets you thinking. We can look at the details later. Here goes . . .

"Fixing it" with your father

Your father is your emotional line of contact to your masculinity. You have to work toward a clear and resolved relationship between yourself and him. You cannot get on with your life successfully until you have understood him, forgiven him, and come, in some way, to respect him. You may do this in conversation with him if he's alive, or in your mind if he is now dead. Unless you do this work, his corpse will drag around behind you, and trip you up every time you make a move!

Finding sacredness in your sexuality

You have to find out how to be not just comfortable but transformed and fulfilled in your sexuality. Sex will either be a sleazy and obsessive part of your life or a sacred and powerful source of well-being. There isn't any in between. First you must relocate your sexual energy in yourself, instead of giving it away to women. Then you need to learn the art of the dance—the specific role a man must take to make the sexual tension between male and female a loving and positive one.

Meeting your partner on equal terms

Anyone can get a partner—the trick is keeping them. To do

this you must learn how to meet your partner, and in fact all women, as different but equal beings. This means respecting her but respecting yourself, too. In order to have a successful marriage that lasts, you will sometimes need to be able to debate fiercely and to do so in a safe and focused way so that problems get solved. In a modern marriage, soft men are boring, and yet bullies drive self-respecting women away. Today's man has to learn to both communicate his own feelings, and listen to those of his partner. This takes great balance!

Engaging actively with your kids

You can't parent from behind a newspaper and you can't leave it all to your partner either—because it isn't fair, and because a woman doesn't have all the ingredients needed. You will have to get the "tough-tender" balance right with your children. This is important for sons, for the reasons we've mentioned, and for daughters, who depend on fathers for a considerable amount of their self-esteem and their whole template for relating to the opposite sex.

Learning to have real male friends

Being a man is almost impossibly hard at times, and to do it you will need emotional support from other men. Other men can also help you find out how to live, through sharing their experiences good and bad. They can save you years of needless errors.

They can relieve the suffocating dependency you may have on your partner as your only confidante. They can also provide a community of men for your teenage sons and daughters to experience and so make up the gaps that you can't always fill. And having male friends is invigorating. They remind you to loosen up, and they deflate your ego every chance they get!

Finding your heart in your work

You must find work you can believe in, so that the time and energy of your working life is spent in a direction where your heart lies. It isn't enough just to make a living. The real work of men is to support and protect life and to build toward a better world. If you don't believe in your own work then the inner contradictions of it will slowly start to kill you. Since most jobs today are for heartless corporations whose goals we do not believe in, this is a huge issue.

Freeing your wild spirit

The god of men does not dwell in the suburbs or the office buildings. Inner steadiness does not come from achievements or possessions. You will need to find a spiritual basis for your inner life that is specifically masculine and based in nature, which connects you to the earth you live on. As you grow older this will be your source of strength and harmony, freeing you from fear and dependency on others.

That's the list. The sequence is not fixed. Some may already be accomplished in your life, others current, and still others seemingly insurmountable. Some of these points may puzzle or surprise you, some may strike a chord. By now you might be full of questions. If so, that's good. This book is devoted to exploring these ideas and to spelling out their practical implications. All of the above steps are necessary for you to progress to full manhood. So let's get started.

IN A NUTSHELL

• The software of how to be male has been lost in our culture.

• Gradually in the last ten years, the elements are being rediscovered or redesigned so we can begin to learn healthy manhood.

• Seven roads to manhood are covered in this book; healing the father-wound, becoming sexually enlivened, relating to women as equals, becoming an involved father, having real male friends, finding the heart in your work, and finding your spirit.

4 You and Your Father

THERE IS A special survey that I "administer" whenever I work with groups of men. I've given this test in China, New Zealand, Scotland, Colorado, with dreadlocked young men in a rainforest camp, and with British politicians in the Houses of Parliament. The survey has only one question: "How do you get along with your father?"

The results are almost always the same. An incredible one third of the men will say, (with some feeling and aggravation evident in their body language) that they rarely even speak to their father. Their relationship is non-existent. They barely if ever see him. This is a shocking situation, by any measure.

Around another 30 percent say that they have a somewhat "prickly" or difficult relationship. If they do spend time with their father, it's hostile and tense. Father and son easily hurt each other with wounding comments or awkward exchanges. Wives and mothers will point this out to them, will question it, or express sadness that it is so. But there seems to be no way of stopping the pattern. And anyhow, it's all *his* fault!

Yet another 30 percent fare somewhat better—they visit their father or phone him regularly, show up for family get-togethers, go through the motions of being a good son. This group look like they have a good relationship, but that isn't exactly true. They have an *involvement* with their father— but not an *intimacy*—they discuss nothing deeper than lawn-mowers and electric drills. If something important came up—the illness of their mother, money problems, a divorce, they would have a lot of trouble dealing with it. And there's something even worse about this relationship—it's boring!

There is one small group remaining, in case you've been doing your math. About one man in ten, if asked about his father, breathes in a slow deep breath, his eyes shine a little, and leans back in his chair. "My father is great" they say. "He's the best." And they mean it. They find their father to be an anchor, a backstop, a lifelong source of support, good sense, comfort, and encouragement. He might be old-fashioned, or have different views, but there is warmth and pride flowing both ways. Men who have this kind of relationship with their dads have a different kind of life as a result. We all—men and women—feel sustained and buoyed up as we go through our lives, if we know that our father thinks we are great. (We need this from our mother too, but she usually lets us know.) How tragic that only a small number of men have the ease and quiet pride that comes from knowing "my father loves me and is proud of me." How different the world would be if we all— men and women—could count on this. And of course, the big question—Is it possible to reach such a place with your own father, when at the present you belong to one of the three other groups?

THE BIG TALK WITH DAD

Where you stand with your father, and with older men in general, is an important question—in fact your happiness as a man is profoundly affected by the answer. Manhood, it turns out, isn't something you achieve on your own, but through connection—both to the world of women and of men. Half of this equation isn't enough. Unless you can connect to the inherited masculinity of generations of older men, you are like a phone without a socket. Unless your father, and hopefully several other significant older men are present in your life, then thousands of years of masculine culture is missing for you.

Whether your father was an actual presence, or a notable absence in your life growing up, your masculinity—unconsciously and whether you like it or not—is based on his. Most men realize (with alarm) that their father's mannerisms, stances, and even words are deeply a part of them and could leap out at any time. If you are at war with him in your head, you are at war with masculinity itself. In fact, you are hopelessly divided against yourself.

It's important at some stage of your life to have, if you can possibly organize it, a profound conversation or series of conversations with your father. Only by doing this can you get an understanding of his inner world, his reasons, his failures, and his successes. Unless you take this step, you will always be building your own manhood on shifting sands—on guesswork and childhood impressions that were never the whole story. You will be acting reactively, rather than constructively and from a free stance. Other older men and women may supplement what you didn't get from your father—and their role is vital—but his primary place in your life will still be there. Even if he was an alcoholic, a wife beater, a child abuser, even if he ran out and you never met him, your biological father still matters. Until you come to terms with him he will haunt you from the inside, where he lives on in you and your sons and daughters for ever. A scary thought.

HOW YOUR FATHER COLORS YOUR LIFE

One of the ways your father will "hang around" is by coloring your attitude to all older men. Perhaps you don't trust older men because you couldn't trust your father. Perhaps you are rebellious to authority in general because your father was unloving and harsh. Perhaps you try to impress older men because you couldn't please your father. Perhaps you have been feeling superior to older men, that you can do without them, or can outsmart them. The fact is though, until you reach a place where you can feel love and respect for your father and also receive the love and respect of older men, *you will remain a boy.*

I have spoken to men whose fathers died or abandoned their mothers and were never seen again. I've also talked to many men whose fathers committed suicide. This leads to deeply buried hurt and confusion, since the message a little child always takes is "What did I do to make him leave? What's wrong with me?"

Men can suppress this pain by hard work and denial but will still be prone to outbursts of deep distress, often masked by anger. Sometimes men decide this situation cannot be allowed to continue. They make the journey into their father's past, which often means making a real-life journey across the country or across the world. It has led men to visit the site of POW camps or battlefields in Europe, to talking to contemporaries of their father in the country they emigrated from, looking up long-lost relatives, and through all these ways, making a deep personal journey to heal the emptiness and understand the whole picture and so let themselves and their fathers "off the hook." The journey can be into your own memory banks, as long-forgotten incidents and experiences surface. Listening to other men's stories helps to trigger this, since our childhoods were often cut from the same cloth.

Sometimes dreams bring new information, or long-lost memories will surface in other ways. Let me tell you of a personal instance. As a young man in my thirties, I was very focused on the deficiencies of my father, the things he didn't do or offer me especially during my teens, which were a rocky time during which I ran away from home, got into all kinds of risky situations, and had many upheavals. I wished I had gotten a better dad. Almost anyone would do. My psychotherapy training fed into this—parent-blaming being a major industry at the time! One evening I was watching a movie my partner had brought home, which she felt might interest me. I don't recall the name of the movie, but it featured a father and son who at one point in the story had a fist fight by the freeway at night! So it was kind of intense. As the movie ended and the credits began to roll, I started to cry—something I had rarely ever done since childhood. It was not just quiet weeping either, but huge gulping sobs that spasmed through my chest and belly. I was suddenly remembering specific positive things my father had done when I was very young. I remembered his keeping me warm inside his coat at a football game, and how good that felt. I remembered a time I caught chicken pox when I was about five, and crying in the night with the sores and fever, and my dad coming and bathing the sores with cool lotion. I remember when he would hold my hand as we walked out on snowy nights when I was about six, as we crisscrossed the neighborhood delivering betting slips to his cronies around the town. I had blocked out these memories because they didn't match the story in my head that my dad was never close. Now they came flooding back—along with grief for the closeness we had lost through the painful time of my teens. It didn't erase the problems, but it balanced them. And it made me want to seek him out again. The real story was so much more complex, rich, and valuable.

> I had blocked out these memories because they didn't match the story in my head

Coming to terms with your father, having a rounded view of him, is especially important if you are a father yourself, and more so if you are in any kind of leadership role. You will never gain respect, unless you can give it. This means looking again at people who are not perfect, but who have strengths nonetheless. Seeing that there is something to respect in them.

For those of us whose fathers are still alive, the opportunity is still there to do something about reconciling. The American poet Robert Bly tells the following story to many audiences. . . . A man in his early thirties decides to make a phone call long distance. He is making an attempt to bridge the gap that has grown between him and his father. They have had little contact in recent years, and the son has been doing some thinking. When the father answers the phone, the son begins to try to tell him. . . .

"Hi, Dad, it's me."

"Oh. . . . uh huh! Hi, son! I'll go get your mother . . . "

"No, don't get Mom. It's you I want to talk to . . . "

There's a pause, then . . .

"Why? Do you need money?"

"No, I don't need money."

(The audience always laughs at this point).

And the younger man starts on his somewhat rehearsed, but still vulnerable speech . . .

"I've just been remembering a lot about you, Dad, and the things you did for us. Working all those years in your job with the city. I know you hated that job, it didn't do anything for you. But you did it, supporting us, putting me through college. My life is going well now and it's because of what you did to get me started. I just thought about it and realized I'd never really said thanks. . . . "

Silence on the other end of the phone. The son continues. "So I want to tell you. . . . Thanks."

There's a long pause before the father answers.

"You've been drinking????"

Whenever this story is told, the audience laughs out loud, but the men laugh with eyes wet and shining.

WHAT FATHERS WAIT TO HEAR

Every father, however much he puts on a critical or indifferent exterior, will spend his life waiting at some deep level to know that his sons and daughters love and respect him. Make sure you absorb this point—he will spend his *life* waiting. This is the huge power you hold in your hands, just by virtue of being someone's child. Everyone these days accepts that a parent has the power to crush a child's self-esteem. Few realize that a child, in time, holds the same power in reverse. Parents wait, however defensively, for their children to pass judgment. That's how life is.

A friend of mine had a father who was "impossible"—he walked out of the room, sometimes right out of the house, if ever somebody tried to talk to him about matters of importance. My friend had often attempted to talk over his childhood, to heal wounds and misunderstandings, but the old man had always evaded him. This old man developed cancer and was in the hospital, hooked up to tubes in and out of him. My friend received word that his father was dying, and flew to be at his side. He walked into the hospital, closed the door of his father's room and said, "I've got you now!" He began to tell his father how angry he was about all the things that had happened, what a useless father he was. The old man seemed to revive a little, began to tell about how things had not always gone as he had wished either, how there were things that the younger man had not known about, could not have understood, all those years ago, reasons behind some of the choices that had been made. These revelations lead to more questions, and they talked animatedly for a long time. After a time, a sense of peace came over both the men, and they just sat there. At the end, the two men were holding hands.

It takes courage to have this kind of conversation, and we perhaps should not risk waiting for a death bed scene to get it started. At one stage in my life, furious and desperate, I drove my father to a remote beach and refused to take him home until we talked! He came through very well.

CREATING THE SPACE TO HEAL

Setting up this kind of conversation means being willing to be vulnerable, not in control, fumbling, being wrong. Getting this right will challenge you to the core. The words "I love you" are cheap and easily said, which is part of the reason we hesitate to speak them. It's not the words that matter. But the connection is important, however it is conveyed. Whether it is through a tone of respect, a liking for each other's company, a hug, or a touch, you will find your own way. Eventually though, to remove any doubt, you have to tell your father (and your mother) what you feel and all that you feel, or else just go on pretending.

A lot is at stake. If you are a man and you run from this confrontation, then your father will die hurting and you will lose a precious opportunity. It's been said that many men go to their graves convinced that they have been an inadequate human being. They know they have failed to win the respect of their children. How bitter this must feel. So who should make the first move? It is possible that your father will seek you out one day to deal with this himself. It is possible but unlikely. You are the one who has the benefit of the insights of our generation. You are the one reading this book. You are the one who has grown bigger by standing on his shoulders. It might be up to you to make the first move.

YOUR MOTHER'S VIEW

You may have built-in prejudices against your father, for a surprising reason. Very often and sometimes with the best of intentions, a mother will turn her son against his father. Again, Robert Bly has a brief and powerful story (in the video lecture "A Gathering of Men") which, when he tells it, lands in an audience like an emotional hand grenade. It's about a man who decides to make up his own mind about his father:

> At about thirty-five, he began to wonder who his father really was. He hadn't seen his father in about ten years. He flew out to Seattle, where his father was living, knocked on the door and when his father opened the door, said, "I want you to understand one thing. I don't accept my mother's view of you any longer."
> What happened?
> The father broke down into tears and said, "Now I can die."
> Fathers wait. What else can they do?

If you're a father with an adult son, reading this book, then why wait? If you're a son with a living father, then the challenge is clear. Are you ready to make that journey? Often, to start with, you don't feel much love for your father, much less respect him. Perhaps you hate him. If there are differences between you, then these cannot be ignored. Don't pretend things are okay. It simply won't work and you will feel cheapened. Differences have to be dealt with (more on this later).

If you fail to investigate your father, with compassion and an open mind, then you may be plagued all your life with a sense of hopelessness, that perhaps deep down you are defective because you come from a defective father. As you start to get to know him as a human being, then you may come to see that no one is all bad, and you may start to be more compassionate to yourself as well. In a curious way, this is the start of courage. It's the same with a father who everyone hails as a saint. Knowing you can never measure up, you carry this like a weight around your neck. Discovering that he was not perfect at all, in fact all too human, can free you to be the kind of good man that *you* want to be.

Finding an understanding of their father's position is a necessary work for all sons, if they are ever to graduate as men.
Respect (love mixed with admiration) is the food of the male
soul. Sons have to "discover" respect for their fathers, which
is not the same as pretending it. They also need to receive
respect from their fathers.

THE APPROVAL ALL SONS CRAVE

In a superb Christian book on men's development, called
Healing the Masculine Soul, Gordon Dalbey, a minister, tells
this story. . . . A young man, in his late twenties, writes to his
father. The young man is a successful professional, but plagued
with insecurities and hurt by the difficult times he had with
his father through his teens. In his letter he is direct and to the
point. He asks his father whether he loves him. A letter comes
back in reply, courteous and formal in tone: "I love all my
kids—you should know that."

The young man feels let down, though it takes a while to
figure out why. He eventually realizes he's been short-changed
*and this was what always happened, throughout his child-
hood.* "I love all my kids . . . " is a cop out, it ducks the point
of making a direct one-to-one statement. Direct praise is
avoided. Direct contact is never made. Encouraged by Dalbey,
the son persists. He writes again. He is frightened to do so, but
he takes a chance. Here are the exact words of the father's reply:

> I have to thank you for pushing me with your question. I guess
> I hadn't really thought that deeply about it. But when I did think
> about it, I realized that I do love you, Peter, and I need to say
> that for myself probably as much as you may need to hear it.

Nothing is more powerful in the psychology of childhood
than the need for love and approval. Unless a child receives

clear and tangible demonstrations of these, their spirit will wither like a flower without water. It's as basic as that. I've watched tiny children in hovels in Calcutta dancing for their admiring relatives, who respond with warm applause and hugs. I've also watched western children bring home their report cards from their expensive private school, young faces eager for praise, only to receive cool, critical appraisals from their performance-oriented, uptight parents.

I don't in my heart understand where this parental coldness comes from. When I look at my own kids through certain eyes, the urge to hug them and praise them to the skies is sometimes overwhelming. Clearly these are the world's most wonderful kids! I'm sure all parents feel this—so something must go badly wrong for parents to shut down these natural feelings.

We are programmed to expect and get love from a mother and a father, and one or two other special adults besides. When our natural need for love is fulfilled, it settles into the background and we can simply get on with our life. We have a quiet confidence that has nothing to prove. Unfulfilled, though, the need for approval becomes an obsession. Many of the people who dominate our public life—business tycoons, politicians, and many sports achievers—are driven by this unfulfilled hunger. "See, Dad? See what I can do?" And of course it doesn't work. "But, son, can't you do better?"

> Do you love me, even though I differ from what you expect?

It is always difficult for men of differing generations to reconcile with one another, especially in times of rapid social change, and the changes have been huge all through the twentieth century.

Things get harder still if there is a major difference of orientation—for instance a gay son or lesbian daughter. At heart the issue is really the same: Do you love me, even though I differ from what you expect? I am not the one you dreamed of. The movie *The Sum of Us*, with Jack Thompson and Russell Crowe, is great viewing for any father, however young their son might be, as a way to relax around this issue.

Every parent alive has built up a dream adulthood for their children. It's so important to let go of these dreams should they not work out. Many terrible wounds arise at this time—from fathers who wanted a son and got a daughter; wanted an athlete and got an artist; wanted a musician and got a laborer; wanted Olympic gold and got cerebral palsy. The problem is not the different outcome but the refusal to grieve and then move on—to love what you have got instead of what you wanted.

It might be one of the biggest stretches imaginable for our souls on this Earth—to abandon our shallow, egotistical dreams and to realize how much better our real children are than any fantasy we could have made up.

FIXING IT WITH YOUR FATHER

Clearly, things are best worked out between living fathers and sons. Once you accept this as a necessary step in your own liberation, it comes down to practicalities. Men I talk with often say they avoid starting any real discussion with their fathers for fear of starting a huge fight—of making matters worse. "He's too old to change now," they say. "It's better to let things be." Perhaps many fathers also live in fear that their sons will show up armed with sacks full of blame and criticism of their inadequacy. They are hardly likely to expect a good outcome.

One way is to go in with an open mind. Don't start with your fists up. ("Justify yourself, you sonofabitch!") Wait for the right time. Choose your time—when there is privacy, and time. Wait until your mother is not around. (He has made adaptations in order to live peaceably with her, but that is not the whole of him.) Ask him for the true story about his life and how it was for him during your childhood. Ask him about his work, his life, and the decisions he made. Be nonjudgmental. Try to have no agenda other than understanding. Your father may well be suspicious—waiting for you to spring the trap. Unless you can really be open, you may not get the real story.

Go back further still. Find out what was going on in your father's childhood. Then move on to when he was raising you. The truth—his truth—will often be quite different from your childhood impressions. You are humanizing your father in your own mind by doing this, filling out the picture, letting him off the hook of the role all children cast their parents in.

Some fathers will be totally evasive, walking from the room, refusing point blank to speak. I've known fist fights to develop, but I don't recommend this! Remember the goal— you are breaking down the defenses, not the man. Take it slowly. Some men take their father away camping or fishing for a few days so that things can develop.

A friend of mine in Germany had always known that his father had survived something terrible in World War II. All he knew was that his father had been about eleven when Russian soldiers came to their village; he had never spoken of what happened. The father had always been a remote, tense man; though deeply caring for his children, he only ever showed this indirectly—by what he did, rather than what he said. My friend conceived a plan. He asked his father for help in redecorating his apartment, knowing the father would make the long journey to help. (The apartment was actually not in such bad shape!) They painted and worked alongside each other for five days. In the evenings they went to a local café for meals. On the last day, the father finally began to talk about the war. He recounted a series of events that were truly horrific (there is no need to recount them here). He wept, and the two men put down their brushes and held each other. The old man needed his son to understand what he had been through, what had made him so tense all those years. He was finally ready to do this. It happened because my friend created the time and the place, and was patient, so the two of them could find peace.

SOMETIMES IT'S SIMPLE

The problems between fathers and sons can sometimes be very simple, not traumatic at all. Another friend of mine, Trevor (now in his early fifties), gave this example. When he was a boy, Trevor's father would take him on a paper route by car, each morning. They spent about two hours together each day in a peaceful rhythm of teamwork, as the sun slowly came up and melted the frost. It was his favorite time of the day; he loved the closeness to his father and the feeling of being useful in a man's world. Then one day, his father was offered a chance to leave his day job (which he hated) and be a partner in the news agency that owned the paper route. To his son's dismay, he turned it down. The news agency business was sold and the paper route ended.

Trevor stayed angry about this for about thirty years. "He doesn't want to be with me!" When his dad got old and sick, Trevor asked him about it.

"How come you didn't buy into the news agency and keep up the paper route?"

"Because the partner was a gambler and we would have all gone broke."

Simple as that.

Becoming a parent yourself is a sure-fire way to gain more compassion for your own parents. Mark, an engineer in his forties, supported his wife through a "cancer scare" that lasted about two years. At times he would be very uptight and scared and he would often react angrily to his young son, who was just being a normal demanding kid, unaware of his mother's situation. Mark was not yet ready to tell his son about his worries, and the eight-year-old was living in an unknown space—a kind of emotional minefield.

Eventually when his son was ten, Mark joined a men's group. The other men urged him to explain what had happened. His son—who earlier would perhaps have been very worried—was relieved to understand, and proud to be trusted. His behavior and schoolwork both improved. Children often do not know what is going on, and we don't always make the right judgment about when to involve them and when not to. They may just come to the conclusion we don't like them, and keep that conclusion for life.

These are important things to clear up. As you talk to your father, you may find that things fall into place. One of the biggest things is to simply say, "Thanks." There may be many specific memories or instances that you recall as a beautiful part of your growing up. Your father may have no idea that he ever "got it right."

Some families have preserved a kind of mythical consensus that they were always happy and got along just fine. Which of course no family ever really does. You may have real problems because of this, and the barrier to trust is the fact that the real picture is not being faced up to. It is possible to tell your father—without it being an attack—what you hated, what you found terrifying, or how lonely and sad you felt through his lack of appreciation and warmth. He may react angrily. He may just criticize you all over again. Don't give up—you are not a child now. Stay clear-headed. Ask why. Ask to know everything. Eventually, some understanding—some forgiveness, perhaps apology or some perspective—will enter into the air between you. No one can predict or program how this will happen. Prepare to be surprised.

One of the few definites that emerged in twentieth-century psychology was that unfinished business has to be addressed. It isn't always right to "forgive and forget"—to say "They had it tough" or "They were only doing their best" or "They're old now, so why make waves?" This doesn't address the truth nor does it address the part of you that has real hurt that needs to be acknowledged. It isn't possible to forgive what hasn't first been acknowledged. Short-cutting this work patronizes your father and alienates you. Deep down you both know it's a lie, and you just become more distant.

> You want to heal both of you, before it is too late

Remember though, that the goal is to get things right between you. You are not there to get even, to "make him suffer like he made me suffer" or anything like that. That would just spin the wheels of pain around one more time. You are aiming for a resolution that is real and complete. You want to heal both of you, before it is too late.

BURIED TREASURE

Most men find talking about their father an uncomfortable subject and men have succeeded in avoiding it for many generations.

Yet how many men do you know who are like this? As they split the wood, fix the car, or write a check, you can almost hear them muttering in argument with a long-dead ghost: "You're making a mess of that, son!" "Fuck off, Dad!" Forgiving your father—not just by effort of will but by actual understanding of his life—will be one of the most freeing things you ever do.

Some men get very sad at this point because their father is already dead, and the conversations we are suggesting can never take place. It seems that an opportunity has been lost forever. Not true. He is in you and you can begin the process. In imagination, in dreaming, by talking to his gravestone or writing him a letter, you can begin to shift the grief. It is awkward but important. You can go on an actual, personal odyssey—finding out more information, traveling to his place of birth and the locations of significant events in his life, talking to his contemporaries, starting to fill in the missing details. Very often, it helps you to discuss this quest with other men on similar journeys. We all have so much in common and can help to release each other's grief, finding support and clarification at the same time. A surprising amount of feeling flows out with this process, and much health and strength flows in to take its place.

Don't run from the past; it is always, eventually, a treasure trove.

IN A NUTSHELL

- Very few men are close to their fathers.

- Sometimes your life won't work until you go back and heal this relationship. (If you hate your father, you often hate yourself too.)

- Many men are starting to have conversations with their father that lift a load from both men and are the beginning of more joyful living.

- Setting up these conversations takes care and awareness.

- Even if your father is dead or lost, there are steps you can take.

5 Sex and Spirit

HUMAN SEXUALITY, AT its best, is a doorway. It opens into places of laughter and delight, tenderness and exhilaration. It is a huge energy source. It motivates us to communicate with that most difficult and challenging feature of our lives—the opposite sex! It releases us from the ordinary and allows us to glimpse wild nature, alive and free and living in our own body.

That's at its best! Sadly though, for the great majority of men, sex is none of these things at all. For many it is a source of unending misery, frustration, and despair. But it doesn't have to be this way.

The so-called Sexual Revolution of the 1960s had some remarkable and positive effects—but these were not evenly handed out! For women, there was a fundamental shift in self-knowledge and sexual openness. Countless books, workshops, discussions, and programs helped women to get in touch with their bodies, to honor their sexuality, and from that knowledge to confidently communicate their needs and wishes to their partners. Women learned they could initiate, control, and choose the manner of lovemaking. And there was for a time a sense of reverence toward women's sexuality. However, many wise women commenting on this phenomenon today point out that young women are still in deep trouble, because the revolution was only partial, that in fact it was hijacked by darker forces of commercial greed, as well as, let's face it, our own immaturity. Many young people today think that sex is just something like ice cream, or a "need" with no more depth or soul attached to it than going to the bathroom. Worse still, the media and advertising have annexed the message of sexual liberation for their own uses, so that there is now a relentless pressure on young women to see themselves in terms of how they look, and how sexually available they are; that this is their "booty"—their power and their only source of worth.

For men it is even worse. Men may have enjoyed the sexual revolution, there was more sex going on—or at least going on more openly. But nothing in any of this served to break men out of their self-image as simply being sex machines who wanted as much as possible, with as many partners as possible.

THE SHAME CONTINUES

Boys had long grown up receiving no real training in relationships, and in fact getting all kinds of demeaning or negative messages about their deepest feelings.

Today most men are basically still ashamed of their sexual feelings—they feel themselves to be essentially creeps. They are poorly developed as communicators, not really aware of their own inner world. They make love from the lizard part of their brain, which might satisfy a female lizard, but isn't enough for a thinking, feeling woman! The result is poor communication and conflict over sex. It has become almost universal that men and women's sexual relationships reach a point of breakdown. Married couples who in other dimensions of their life can cooperate, share, and trust quite well, still have a miserable time in the bedroom. Only those with great wisdom, patience, and a generous sense of humor manage to navigate these shoals.

Unequal desire develops; coldness and rejection set in. Instead of sexuality being integrated into the whole of life, its difficulties or its absence comes to dominate a man's every waking moment—so that most men under the age of fifty operate more like sex addicts than true lovers—needy, unsatisfied, and obsessed.

No other aspect of male life has been so simultaneously exploited, misunderstood, neglected, and demeaned. As one man wrote to me, "Our penises, which should be winged steeds on which to fly to heaven, now just get used to nail us to the ground."

There is an urgent need to heal the sexuality of men. Fortunately, in the last ten years, something new has begun to happen. Spontaneously in western countries around the globe, thousands of men's groups have formed with a guiding ethos of speaking honestly, from the heart (instead of the usual locker room posing that passed for male sharing in the past). As a consequence, men have begun to understand their sexuality beyond the crass and demeaning stereotype that "men just want one thing." This self-exploration is bringing to light many surprises and insights. Whole new approaches to marital therapy, such as that described by David Schnarch in his book *Passionate Marriage*, treat sex in terms of its *meaning*, instead of just its biological functioning. Only by understanding what sex means to us, and bringing this communication to the bedroom, can we have a chance of sexual joy.

Paradoxically, as men talk more honestly to other men, they are able to begin to talk more honestly to women. This has a cascading effect—the relaxation and trust that grows from being accepted and valued mean that couples are able to have more exuberant and intimate lovemaking as a result. What these men's groups and researchers have discovered, and the implications for sexual healing, will be spelled out in this chapter. The reasons for our sexual problems are largely cultural, and solvable. There is great hope, and scope, for improvement, and you can begin right away.

ARE MOST MEN NON-ORGASMIC?

Male sexuality, especially the nature of the male climax, is grossly misunderstood by men—and women. Columnist Michael Ventura wrote this brilliant analysis:

> . . . certainly the weakest, silliest aspect of feminism—which for the most part has been an overwhelmingly beneficial movement—has been its description of male sexuality. It was a description that assumed a monolithic mono-intentional erection; it was a description that equated the ejaculation of sperm with coming. But there are many secret passageways within an erection. As far as the question of male coming—it is an immense and untried question. Ejaculation is a muscle spasm that many men often feel with virtually no sensation but the twitch of the spasm. To ejaculate is not necessarily to come. Coming involves a constellation of sensations, physical, psychic, emotional, of virtually infinite shadings. Coming may sometimes or often occur at the moment of ejaculation, when it occurs at all. But many ejaculations for many men happen without any sensation of coming.
>
> Until a woman understands this she doesn't know the first thing about male sexuality. Nor do many men. There is ample evidence in face after face that, as there are women who have never come, so there are men who have often ejaculated but never come. And they likely don't know it, as many women never knew it until a few began to be vocal about such things. These men live in terrifying and baffling sexual numbness in which they try the right moves and say the right things but every climax is, literally, an anticlimax. It is no wonder that in time they have less and less connection with their own bodies, and are increasingly distant from the women they want to love.
>
> (From *To Be a Man*, edited by K. Thompson)

This takes some digesting. There are, it seems, orgasms and orgasms. Norman Mailer, in his book *The Prisoner of Sex*, wrote of the difference between "orgasms stunted as lives, screwed as mean and fierce and squashed and cramped as the lives of men and women whose history was daily torture" and contrasts these with others "as far away as the aria and the hunt and the devil's ice of a dive, orgasms like the collision of a truck or coming as soft as snow, arriving with the riches of a king in costume or slipping in the sneaky heat of a slide down slippery slopes."

This represents a delightful variety. (Although there is little mention of closeness, contact, or any other emotional qualities in Mailer's writings. He's still hung up on sensation, not emotion. You get the feeling that it's him and his body, with some woman along for the ride!)

There is more available than just pleasure. Older, experienced partners describe a deep connection that is the real goal of lovemaking—looking soft-eyed into one another's faces, hearts open, bodies relaxed and abandoned, gradually letting go of all defenses in trust of each other and of the natural power that possesses you. The fierceness that is released when you are able to trust. As one woman friend of mine put it, "Once you have made love, then just having sex will never do."

This isn't to say that lovemaking always has to be so intense. But that it can always be a meeting of two human beings—not just (to use family therapist Carl Whitaker's phrase) "a penis and a vagina going out on a date together!"

LOVING AS A WHOLE MAN

The popular term for sexual climax, "coming," is such an interesting choice of word. Who is it that is arriving? Clearly the divinity within each partner enters the room at these times. The everyday sense of self is awed and overtaken by this feeling of being something bigger and better—the truth really, since our everyday sense of who we are is not the whole story. In lovemaking, the god in man meets the goddess in woman and they are taken out of space and time, knowing everything, lost in love. Regaining this sense of spirit in one's sexual life takes application. Like meditation, it's simple and takes years. Yet it can be as simple and as profound as just learning to relax.

John O'Hara, in his novel *Appointment in Samarra,* has one of his characters express it this way:

> I never made love before, I just screwed. But when it happened, it was like nothing I'd ever experienced before. I think I must have blacked out for a second and all I was aware of was some kind of incredible warmth, my whole body was filled with it and I didn't want to leave her or roll away from her. I wanted to get closer to her, very close. I could feel the warmth of her body against mine, soft and gentle and for the first time in my life I stayed in a woman's arms and fell asleep.

Paul Olson, in *Wingspan,* comments on this passage: "What he does with that experience only time will tell. He can deny it in the morning. Or he can enter it fully and never again feel the need to run away."

Clearly, for us to experience this kind of union (what some might call "sacred sex") requires all kinds of readiness, timing, openness, and communication—as well as just good luck! A lot of other things have to be right. It may require years of self examination, fighting over housework, learning to trust, and becoming natural. Yet these years would be clearly well spent. We start life as tender babies and spend our whole life just regaining that absolute openness and trust.

An important and helpful ingredient for total lovemaking is the inclusion of nature—of letting in the signals and rhythms that the natural world sends to our cells to help tune them in. That's what romance means—it means not artificial. Even in terms like "the romance of sail" we are noticing a preference for the natural elements over the man-made environment. The old clichés endure because they are potent triggers. We think of romance as standing on an ocean beach watching the moon rise, of dining by candlelight, of making love on a rug by a fireside or impulsively falling to the ground together in the long grass of the dunes, laughing and pulling off each other's clothes to explore the warm skin beneath. Sex is about going back to nature, giving way to wildness—something you should never get too old for! Romance means bringing a wild heart to an erotic body, "With the naked earth beneath us and the universe above."

MEN AND WHOLE-BODY SEX

Feminism gave women back the power to control their own bodies—and the pleasure of fully being alive to their bodies. Women today can decide for themselves whether and when they want sex and how they want it to be. In the daring first studies of the Fifties and earlier, fewer than 20 percent of women were found to be orgasmic. Learning to become so, and to confidently and routinely let their partners know their needs and desires, was a very major shift.

Like the women of the Victorian era, most men don't know what they are missing. One only has to watch the reptilian grunting and grinding of the men in "adult" movies to realize these guys have never seen or felt a real orgasm. Like the women of the pre-Sixties era, many men, too, are not yet orgasmic—what they think is an orgasm is just a mere ejaculation, which is only a tiny part of the story. The key to feeling more is to place less emphasis on the mechanical outer performance or actions, and more on the inner qualities of sensory and emotional experience. Sex is active, but it's also about noticing. Just as you can eat an orange without even tasting it, sex only touches us as deeply as we let it. We men feel pretty lucky if our partner asks what we would like to do in bed. But the most magical woman is the one who asks what we would like to feel.

Barry Oakley once illustrated the difference between doing sex, and feeling sex, in his column in the *Australian Magazine*—using two contrasting quotations. The first is by Ken Follett, from his blockbuster novel *Night Over Water*:

> *This was not what was supposed to happen, she thought weakly. He pushed her gently backwards on the bed and her hat fell off. "This isn't right," she said feebly. He kissed her mouth, nibbling her lips gently with his own. She felt his fingers through the fine silk of her panties. . . .*

You'll notice straight away that it's all action and adverbs. There is nothing about feeling or inner experience. The passage is mechanical and totally devoid of charm.

Then, for comparison, Oakley quotes D. H. Lawrence, from *Women in Love*:

> *She was with Birkin, she had just come into life, here in the high snow, against the stars. What had she to do with parents and antecedents? She knew herself new and unbegotten, she had no father, no mother, no anterior connections, she was herself pure and silvery, she belonged only to the oneness with Birkin, a oneness that struck deeper notes, sounding into the heart of the universe, the heart of reality, where she had never existed before.*

Okay, it's a little over the top, but so much more alive! The writing works from the inside out—from the real experience. Great writing about sex is rare because this level of aliveness is rare—you had to have experienced what you were writing about. But at least as the reader we can imagine it, and therefore can begin to travel down that road, toward sex that is truly mind-blowing and heart-melting.

The Lawrence quote tells nothing at all about the details. Nothing for little boys to giggle about, since they would simply not understand. These days we inform kids about the mechanics of sex. How do we let them know what the real meaning of it is? One person I know told her curious daughter—it's like the best hug you ever had—but you have to do it with the right person, in the right time and place or it's just a mess. It takes all our poetry, music, art, and a real generosity to do, and still they will have to find out for themselves.

SELF LOVE

Sex therapists and educators encourage masturbation as an important part of learning and maintaining healthy sexuality. In a man's life, self-pleasuring begins in the early teens, long

Perhaps one thing that helps is to teach the young that sex always means something. Therapist David Schnarch asks audiences to close their eyes and remember their best ever sexual experience. He then asks them—WHY was it the best? This question elicits the meaning of the experience—people begin to call out "passionate," "tender," "trusting," "funny," "healing," "free," "honest," "athletic!" Those are the happy memories. When sex is bad—and this is worth explaining to teenagers—it's because the meaning is wrong—sex can be— "routine," "revenge," "substitute," "bored," "pressured," "scoring," "using." It can usually only go well when the meaning is shared and understood by both lovers. Before you have sex with someone, be sure you know what they mean by it.

before we establish relationships with women. On the purely physical level, the purpose of masturbation is simply to ensure that sperm are kept fresh and in healthy production. Most men continue to masturbate during marriage, at those times when it isn't right or possible to make love with their partners, and most healthy men will continue well into old age. It's a long-term interest.

For men who are able to utilize their imagination and capacities for fantasy, masturbation is an exercise in sexual independence and in the development of sensuousness. By not rushing, by experimenting and finding what we like, we become more skillful and alive as lovers. A man may find that he is imagining not just the physical aspects of sex, but also the relationship, the conversation, the mood and context, and so prepares himself for relating to a real woman. On the other hand, if masturbation is furtive, rushed, and shameful, or distorted by dependence on low-grade pornography, or if teenagers do not have the privacy or sense of permission they need, then adolescent masturbation can be a training in over-focused and tense sex, which strongly predisposes them to premature ejaculation, and generally a poor quality of love-making in adult life. By having a playful and happy approach to self-pleasuring, men and their lovers benefit enormously.

For men of any age, the aim in self-stimulation is to create a sense of specialness and atmosphere. In recent decades, masturbation stopped being a mortal sin, but it only moved one notch away—to being a kind of necessary evil. It was permitted—but only to "blow off" excess sexual steam! (It was probably more fun when it was a sin!)

It's important to be leisurely, relaxed, unhurried, and tuned-in to the head-to-toe sensations of arousal—to be more open to the pleasures of before and after. Self-pleasuring, for both men and women, is a kind of apprenticeship. It's an important source of self-awareness—a prerequisite to being good in bed.

It's here that we learn what we like so that we can communicate this to our partner. It's here that we learn to let ourselves be totally receptive (a difficult thing for many men)—surrendering to the sensations, trusting them, allowing one's whole body to receive the loving energy that becomes freely available in sexual exchange.

KEEPING THE MAGIC

Our bodies give us the message from inside: sex is magic! But from the outside—from magazines, playground humor, and perhaps sexual abuse at the hands of older men or women—boys and young men get a sleazy, animal, dirty image of their sexual yearnings. As fathers and mothers we have to work hard to strengthen the positive and fend off the negative messages bombarding our sons. As adult men we have to remind ourselves often that our sexuality, as it is, is wholesome and good. Late one night I heard a radio interview with the publishers of a weekly picture magazine. It was the kind of magazine that has huge breasts pointing out from the cover every week and stories like "Warship discovered on moon" on the inside. The magazine editors joked about the whole culture of the magazine, the stories they got away with and what the readers will tolerate.

Listening to the interview, I often found myself smiling—but wincing at the same time. The reason for the interview was widespread criticism of a recent cover photograph showing a naked woman wearing a dog chain, which had actually prompted some new legislation to restrict display of this material in public view. Most people, rightly, found this cover offensive. The interviewer ended with the predictable question: "Does your magazine cheapen women?"

"No, not really," the editor answered. But then he went on, laughing, "If it demeans anyone, it's the guys who read it!" Exactly.

FINDING A BALANCE

Parents in more puritanical times wanted to keep their children ignorant of sex—preferably forever. Sexual information has made a happier, more sane and honest world, freer of the perversions and cruelties that ran thickly under the veneer of nineteenth century propriety.

Today's parents don't object to information—it's misinformation that angers us. We want our children enjoy their sexuality. We want this to happen, though, in a timely way, keyed to their level of growth and maturity. Many experts have noted that exposure of children to the media robs them of their childhood—it frightens and overwhelms.

A child's innocence can be stolen by an abuser, but it can be knocked around badly by an ill-timed video, too. We have to be careful, and the media need to clean up their act or face a growing parent boycott.

The biggest problem with pornography (or so called erotica) is that it is so third rate—almost demoralizing. We need some way (as the Japanese once used their "pillow books") to convey to our kids what is really going on inside two people in love. As a young man, I saw the movie *Coming Home* with Jane Fonda and Jon Voigt, which included a very moving love scene, made more special by the fact that Voigt played a wheelchair bound Vietnam vet. It was not especially graphic, yet it was intense and magical. I knew, at fourteen, that I wanted to go there.

THE DARK SIDE

Cheapening isn't the only risk. There is a deeper danger for boys and men in the power of sex. If this energy doesn't flow in a good direction, it can sometimes go in a very bad one. There has been a major and justified focus in feminism on the capacity of men to hurt and harm in the sexual arena—to exploit, harass, rape, and kill. This isn't a peripheral concern.

Child sexual abuse, to choose just one example, is horrifically widespread and does inestimable damage to millions of people's lives. "All men are animals" isn't an explanation or a cure for this. We urgently have to explore male sexual development, to find out how a healthy energy can become so badly misdirected.

The following extract was written by Jai Noa, a physically disabled man who, in his crippled state, observed that he was quickly turning into a creep. He then made an astonishing leap from examining his own condition, to noticing that in our society this process happens to all men to some extent. Almost all of us feel romantically crippled at some time. Given the media messages sent to men about sex, in the constant use of sexually posed women in advertising—the look-but-don't-touch culture—we can easily start to see our sexuality as loathsome and so begin to incubate a desire to make women suffer in "revenge." In Noa's own words:

> I use the idiom "creep" in a very special sense. "Creep" refers to the ashamed sexuality of most men, which is an inescapable fact of our social life and one which each of us must confront sooner or later. It is ironic that if there is an almost universal manner in which men share a common crippledness, it is in the realm of sexual expression. . . .
>
> A creature of low self-esteem, the creep feels he cannot develop sustained intimate friendships with others. Despairing of intersubjective happiness, he takes the other [the woman] as an object to exploit as best he can. This is a cynical attempt to validate himself through domination. The delightful joys of erotic pleasure are turned into their opposite by a guilt-ridden quest for power. The creep then is a voyeur, a pornophile, and an exhibitionist. He enjoys not only invading the sexual space

> *of others, but also a feeling that his penis has the power to cause a reaction, even if only one of discomfort or disgust.*
>
> *The heterosexual male creep tries to reduce all women to whores, i.e. to what he thinks of as dirty sluts, who are so low they would fuck someone as contemptible as himself (and thereby elevate him!). He may cruise bars or parties in search of a drunken easy lay. In his masturbation fantasies he chooses a woman who is too good for him and envisions her as a slave of sexual passion.*
>
> *The creep is a man who fails to live up to the romantic ideal and who feels crushed, bitter and resigned to this failure. And since most men suffer defeat in the romantic meritocracy, at one time or another, the cripple can find his identity partially located in the world of men. Increasingly, during his teenage years and for an indefinite period of time thereafter, the cripple can find a bond with any men who indulge in misogyny.*

There is nothing crippled about this man's grasp of language! When I first read this essay, "The Cripple and the Man," I sat for a long time in silence. It's possible that Noa has answered one of the social problems of our time. Let's just pull out a key sentence: "Despairing of intersubjective happiness, he takes others as an object to exploit as best he can." In other words, despairing of ever winning anyone's love and closeness, the man who becomes a creep prefers to have the upper hand. Here we have laid open before us the rapist, the child molester, the pornography addict, the serial killer, and the wife beater. We also have Everyman, struggling to feel okay about his wants and desires in a seeming "one-down" position with women—knowing well the feelings expressed in the Dr. Hook song, "Girls can get it any time they want." This is more than just a problem of sexual confidence. Many men confuse sexual rejection with outright rejection—of themselves, and their lovability—so feel double the pain. (It may spread to other aspects of their performance—their earning capacity, physique, and so on.)

All human beings need to feel loved. To be valued as we are, treated with kindness, and to experience daily intimacy. Since most men come to women with such a deep lack of inner worth, they will be tempted—instead of risking rejection as an equal—to use their strength, their sneakiness, their money, and other power plays to impose their needs. Women pay a great price for this. It's a double tragedy. The whole of the prostitution industry relies on the emotional impoverishment of men, so many of whom feel more comfortable buying "pretend" love than dealing with the complexities of the real thing.

> A creep . . . has abandoned the difficult path of intimacy, for the safer one of exploitation

SEXUAL ABUSE AND RAPE

For most men, their perceived lack of sexual power is just depressing. But for men who have been badly abused by their mothers or fathers, and taken into their being the "hurt-or-be-hurt" ethos, it becomes more dangerous. "If you can't get love, get even" becomes this person's inner dynamic.

The rapist knows his victim is helpless and derives pleasure from this. The child molester can only feel good in a position of total power and control. He feels safer this way. Why risk rejection from an adult when you can control a child? There are other complicating factors: often aggression and arousal have been mislinked by the unfortunate training ground of his childhood. Some abusers soothe the memory of the abuse in their own childhood by switching the roles around. It isn't possible to think about these things without one's skin beginning to crawl, but for the sake of women and children everywhere we have to face them.

If we define sexual abuse in its broadest sense, to include indecent exposure, and unwelcome sexual touching, then around one in six children in our society is sexually abused at some time, usually by a boy or man who is part of their family or social circle. Sometimes of course, it is much more invasive than this. In the course of his career, an abusive man may have access to dozens of children, grandchildren, friends, cousins. The damage to the emotional well-being of these children, unless concerted healing intervention takes place, is life-long. Suicide, anorexia, alcoholism, marital problems, drug addiction, depression, and abusiveness to one's own children are just a few of the symptoms.

The violation these men commit is inexcusable, but starts to become comprehensible. A creep isn't a different kind of man—just one who has abandoned the difficult path of intimacy for the safer one of exploitation. We all hover at times on the brink of creephood. We must turn away from going down that road.

HOW WE RAISE OUR KIDS

Prevention in the long-term comes down to how we raise our kids. People who grow up in safety have self-worth and do not need to hurt others. Our first commitment as men must be to never act in a sexual way with children. Children must know, with total confidence, that they will not be mistreated and will not have their sexuality warped by domination and violence.

Surprisingly, perhaps the most important thing we can do as parents is to give up smacking and hitting as forms of punishment, and find better ways of getting cooperation. Children who feel physically safe with their parents, who have not had their psychic boundaries kicked in by adult moods and invasions, are vastly more resistant to abuse, and certainly more likely to tell you if it happens.

The third step is providing young people—the high-risk group for both abuse and becoming abusers—with a sense of belonging. This comes from the involvement of other adults who care and actively teach us. Young men in particular are often made to feel like outsiders in society, and so they act like outlaws. Right now we give young men too little attention. Unless the young man looks like he's becoming a sports star, no older man is interested in him. Boys who succumb excessively to peer-group pressure invariably have weak or absent fathers and no uncles or father-figures to take up the slack. Perhaps boys who participate in gang rapes should have their fathers go to jail along with them. A recent crime conference was told that young people should not live away from adults until they are in their mid-twenties. Before that point, they simply do not have the inner structure to handle independent living.

Boys drift into gangs because they instinctively seek leadership. The gang leader—a year older or a few inches taller—is not equipped to lead them in good directions. (Ghetto boys also join gangs for sheer self-defense because to fail to do so would be suicidal. The gang is their only protection, since the adults have long since lost control.) The gang exacts a price—it takes away your individuality. In the gang world, there is intense conformity based on fear. If you are different, you are not a man and will be persecuted, reviled, beaten up, even killed. (Yet among real men, difference is celebrated.) In such gangs, talk about girls has to be tough, exploitive. If you have no sexual experience, you fabricate some! To show involvement with or tenderness to a girl indicates weakness.

BEING SECURE IN YOUR SEXUAL IDENTITY

Support and help from those of your own gender is essential to making you secure in your sexual identity (the chapter on initiation, "The Wild Spirit of Man," pursues this further). Sex is an inward, personal thing as well as a meeting of man and woman. For a young man to relate to a young woman successfully, he must first be comfortable with himself as a man. Yet this is rarely so. To be successful as a lover, one must first see oneself as lovable, able to receive and give tenderness, as the possessor of a "magical soul and a powerful heart."

Robert Bly stresses the need for young men to know that "sexual energy is good, that animal heat, fierceness and passionate spontaneity is good." With this confidence, there is less aggression or competitiveness—no need to put women down. When you can accept your extravagant, fierce yearnings then you can be unashamed and free of the need to dominate. If your desired woman wants you, then that's great. If she doesn't, then that's okay. Someone else certainly will.

When a man has his inner esteem sorted out—with quiet confidence instead of arrogance—then he can approach an adult woman as an equal, without the need for power or control. He is neither over-shy nor over-aggressive. He can enter the dance of love with pride.

OWNING YOUR SEXUAL CHARGE

There remains one last monster to wrestle. This one has always been with us but, in our society, with its constant media bombardment, it has grown into a large and many-clawed beast.

Women hold such visual and tactile magic for men that it is easy to make the serious mistake of handing one's power over to them. They become the golden woman, the goddess. From Marilyn Monroe to Madonna, our psyche seems to need this mythical figure.

Gordon Dalbey, in *Healing the Masculine Soul*, puts it like this:

> The so-called Playboy philosophy, for example, focuses on the enticing Playmate. The good news of the Playboy gospel is that the woman confers masculinity on the reader by sexually arousing him with her "come-on" posture. In reality, however, the reader has simply yielded his manly initiative to the woman. . . . He has given his masculine spirit over to the goddess and, thus, lost it.

In seeing women as the holders of sexual attraction—as having power over men's desire—men actually give away their own sexual energy. We put women on a pedestal and then resent them for being there. We have to become aware that sexual attraction lies not in the way a woman looks, but in the way we choose to look at a woman. A man's life goes a whole lot better when he realizes that he is turning himself on and that he is a mind with a penis, not the other way around!

> No one arouses us. We arouse ourselves, no matter how convincingly we project such a capacity onto another. Men are not bewitched by women, but are bewitched by their own hoping-to-be engorged appetites, or more precisely, by their unwitting animation of and submission to such appetites, particularly those that promise some pleasurable numbing.
> —Robert Masters, "Ditching the Bewitching Myth" in *To Be a Man*

> Men say their penises have minds of their own, but men are geniuses at avoiding responsibility.
> —Richard Rhodes in *Making Love*

This misconception usually begins in adolescence. The culture of the soft-porn magazine provides a kind of schizophrenic split between the compliant, provocative perfection of the glossy image and the awkward, human, not-so-simple business of relating to real girls. As one writer in *XY Magazine* put it so plaintively, "The pictures never loved me back." The girlie magazine ethos tells a young man, "this is all you really want"—and yet delivers no warmth, no faithfulness, just a wisp of pleasure and then a long emptiness.

FACING DOWN THE STALLION

Minister and counselor Gordon Dalbey, in his book *Healing the Masculine Soul*, whom we've already quoted earlier, tells a striking tale about freeing oneself from sexual manipulation. A young married man comes to him for advice because a woman at work has been seeking him out with tales of her husband's cruelty. They are spending more and more time together and she is becoming increasingly seductive (or he is becoming attracted to her—depending where you locate the responsibility).

Dalbey explores the man's childhood and finds a pattern common to men in this situation. The man's father was considerably older than his mother, and was a remote type of man, who died while the young man was still in his early teens. The boy had always been his mother's comforter and confidant, more so after his father's death. So by the time he entered adulthood, he had already learned that comforting women—with subtle, sexual overtones—was his role in life. In a nutshell, his father's abandonment and his mother's psychic incest had set him up for just such a role.

Dalbey continued to counsel the man over several sessions. Fortunately for the story, the man owned horses, and one morning an incident occurred which had direct bearing on his situation. A stallion, which had broken through a fence from his neighbor's property, was about to start mating with his mares. He found himself face to face with the highly excited, large black horse, armed only with a fence picket. He held his ground and herded the stallion back. Then (surprise, surprise!) he discovered that he could also face down the young woman who was coming (on) to him at work. She was furious and hurt, but in the end she sought help from a woman counselor instead. She later thanked him for not playing a game that would have harmed them both.

The psychic incest that can occur between mothers and sons is rarely talked about, yet it can do enormous damage when a mother makes her son into a husband substitute, even just at a verbal level. The melodramas some men create for themselves with affairs, conquests, and love triangles lose some of their glamour when one realizes that they are still trying to "make it with Mama!"

There will always be flirtation, temptation, and the potential for misuse of sex. The really mature men are those who know they are in charge of their own sexuality. They have "corralled the stallion," to use Dalbey's phrase. Not castrated, just corralled, so you can take it where you want it to go. Men who have learned this bring a kind of inner calmness to their encounters with women which, far from being dulling, is erotic and tantalizing to women in itself. Women are looking for this very capacity in a man. Someone who is capable of steady, fervent pursuit—not an oversized baby wanting to hang from their breast! Harlequin novelists earn millions by acknowledging this facet of the feminine psyche—the irresistibility of a man who is willing to rein back his energy for the right time and place.

But that's enough horsing around!

IN A NUTSHELL

- Don't mistake ejaculation for orgasm. Begin to explore increasing your relaxedness and awareness before, during, and after lovemaking. Consider the possibility that there is vastly greater pleasure available, not from what happens on the outside but from what is allowed by you on the inside.

- Sex isn't a separate part of you. Your heart, spirit, mind, and body need to be along for the ride. Sex is a spiritual practice, capable of transforming your whole outlook and refreshing your sense of glory in being alive.

- Deep sexual pleasure of the kind described above only occurs in a relationship with great emotional trust. This may take years to attain. It's worth the effort.

- Tell your teenagers—that sex always means something. Before you have sex with someone, be sure you know what it means to both of you.

- Masturbation is an essential and healthy part of men's

sexuality throughout life. It is the way we develop appreciation of ourselves and our sensory potential, and realize that we own our own sexual energy.

• Exploitive pornography (as opposed to respectful erotica), prostitution, much advertising, rock videos, and the like degrade men just as much as women. They imply that cheap thrills are all we want and all women offer. Don't be fooled.

• You have to guard against "creepification"—the temptation to choose power over women—rather than the risky and vulnerable path of meeting them as equals. Once you are proud of your gender and your sexuality you will not be afraid to risk rejection, and won't need to force or coerce women into sex. Neither will you abuse children.

• Women don't turn you on. You turn yourself on, by the way you focus on women. Knowing this means you have a choice.

OTHER VOICES

Part of me lived outside my body—outside of emotion and feeling, cynical and hard, believing nothing, trusting nothing and no one. . . . Somewhere along the way . . . the split healed, at least in lovemaking. It felt as if a dense, muffling integument had been peeled away.

Instead of a compacted sensation localized in my groin, my ears roared, my skin flushed, my eyes dimmed, my innards loosened and flowed, and I was one instead of two. I felt boluses of semen moving up through the root and shaft of my penis like Roman-candle charges and then my entire body exploded and I wasn't two or one, I was none and everything. I was there and everywhere at once.

—Richard Rhodes

[The men she had known] . . . waited until dark, they drank to get their courage up, they laid on some perfunctory foreplay, and then they fucked, and whatever happened for the woman happened within that narrow range. I've got mine, now you get yours. They didn't even work to enlarge their own pleasure; once sheathed they drove more or less straight to ejaculation. I'm not surprised they had trouble getting it up and keeping it there.

It's appalling that men willing to invest thought and energy in learning a sport . . . won't invest thought and energy in learning how to play generously at sex. On the evidence, far too many men are sexually selfish and self-centered, reverting in the intimacy of the bedroom to mommy's darlings, taking rather than giving, not required, as girls are required from early childhood, to pay attention to needs other than their own.

—Richard Rhodes

If one appreciates the harmonies of strings, sunlight on a leaf, the grace of the wind, the folds of a curtain, then one can enter the garden of love at unexpected moments. Moreover, after a man or woman has fallen in love, the leaf looks better, turns of phrase have more grace, shoulders are more beautiful. When we are in love, we love the grass, and the barns, and the lightpoles, and the small main streets abandoned all night.

—Robert Bly

My mouth on her body, my tongue savoring her crevices, was like plunging my face into a bowl of ripe summer fruits and inhaling their mingled fragrances— peaches, apples, pears. All of her was fresh. All of her was beautiful.

—Richard Rhodes

The erection, which the feminist and the macho alike have seen as such a one-note, one-purpose organ, is less a sword than a wand.

—Michael Ventura in *Shadowdancing*

6 Men and Women

THERE ARE THREE things men need to understand if they are to get along with women:

1 Meeting your partner as an absolute equal, without seeking to intimidate her or being intimidated by her.

2 Knowing the essential differences in male and female sexuality and so mastering "the art of the chase."

3 Realizing your partner is not your mother and so making it through "the long dark night" when love doesn't happen.

Intrigued? Well, here we go.

MAN AS A LOVABLE DOPE

There's little doubt that up until the 1950s, it was easy for men to be bullies.

They held the reins of power and money. They were bigger, and violence was thought to be a private matter. In recent times though, the average man is something of a wimp. Most modern men, when faced with their wife's anger, complaints, or general unhappiness, simply submit, mumble an apology, and tiptoe away. If they grumble, they do so into their beards. For the most part they act conciliatory and apologize for being such dopes.

"I'm sorry, dear!" (If they accumulate enough "frequent flee-er points" from this swallowed pride, though, they may well cash them in for an affair or a desertion—just to even the score).

In the media, the loveable idiot has become a universal male stereotype for many decades, from Dagwood strip cartoons through the Flintstones to the "Bill Cosby Show." Everywhere you look around, the "husband-as-a-lovable-dope" is an agreed-upon type.

Real life, though, doesn't work like the sitcoms. The millions of men who adopt this stance find that it rarely, if ever, leads to happiness. Women with dopey husbands are not happy—they actually become *more* dissatisfied, more complaining. Often without even realizing why, a woman finds herself becoming a nag—for a simple reason. Deep down, women want to engage with someone as strong as them. They want to be debated with, not just agreed with. They hunger for men who can take the initiative sometimes, make some decisions, let them know when they are not making sense. It's no fun being the only adult in the house. How can a woman relax or feel safe when the man she is teamed with is so soft and weak?

In therapy I have talked to many strong, capable feminist women who tell me that they have finally found the sensitive, caring, new age man they *thought* they wanted and they are *bored stiff!* They are starting to drive slowly past building sites, wondering whether to whistle!

Men are not unaware of their failures in the relationship stakes. Whenever a group of men in their thirties and forties gathers, it soon emerges how many have been badly wounded. In therapy groups and self-help courses today, it's the men who are in tears. Whether they show their sadness openly, or put on a belligerent front, it's the same thing. They know they are failing to satisfy the woman in their life, they have failed to keep their relationships together and don't know what they have done wrong.

It's the hardest thing a man has to do, to hold this balance of being strong, but not a tyrant, soft, but not a wuss. In Holland and Australia, a program called Rock and Water is taught to school-boys to help them avoid and prevent abuse and violence. The name is brilliant, and the method is implicit in the name. Know when to hold firm. Know when to give in, listen, and speak.

HOW TO STAND UP TO YOUR WIFE

Though it may surprise many male readers to know it, women are only human. This means they are sometimes dead right and sometimes completely wrong. Most men are caught up thinking women are either devils or saints and miss this simple point. Women are normal, fallible human beings. So it follows that being married to one you also have to keep your head on straight. You cannot just drift along and let them decide every-thing, which some men do. Marriage is not an excuse to stop thinking. Not only can your wife be wrong, or immature, per-verse, prejudiced, competitive, or stubborn (just like you), some-times you and she just will see things differently. What is right for her may be wrong for you—it's as simple as that.

Being in a relationship means compromise on many things, but it also means knowing who you are, which in turn means knowing what core principles and values you won't give up on. John Lee, in his classic book *At My Father's Wedding* puts it like this:

I'll compromise on where we live, where we eat, how many children we have, what movie we see, where our children will go to school, but not on matters that jeopardize my soul—I need you to stop drinking in this house. I need the abuse to stop. I demand safety. I need to be nurtured. I need love. I need to express my anger. I need you to express yours. I need mutual respect and equality. I will not settle for less than what I know I deserve, which is health. I will not compromise my recovery to be in a relationship.

Partners in a relationship frequently misunderstand each other—and this does not decrease after years of being together. Human beings grow and change, and have to keep updating. Women's experience of life is very different from men's. Our psychology, our biology, our conditioning only partially overlap. How can women understand us, unless we explain ourselves to them? That doesn't mean you can't get along, but you do have to keep negotiating! Being falsely agreeable doesn't help either of you. Prepare for many long, patient debates!

WHEN MEN WON'T FIGHT

I have heard so many women say in frustration, "My husband won't fight with me, he won't even argue. He just walks away." Perhaps the husband walks away because he doesn't want to get physical like his father used to do. Or perhaps he had a nagging mother and a weak father. He has never known a man with backbone. To have a happy marriage, a man has to be able to state his point of view, to debate, to leave aside hysteria and push on with an argument until something is resolved.

Gordon Dalbey tells of a woman who phoned him after he had counseled her husband. "It's obvious Sam's getting stronger, speaking up for himself and letting me know how he feels," she said, hesitating. "I know I've always wanted him to be that way . . . but . . . I guess there's a part of me that kind of enjoyed having the upper hand and being able to manipulate him into doing what I wanted. I want to be strong enough myself so that I don't do that anymore."

It's to her credit that this woman is willing to give up some of her power in order to experience a really equal relationship, based on intimacy and negotiation, not on emotional dominance.

THE GUARDIAN

There is a part of every healthy person's internal repertoire that we could call "the Guardian." The Guardian does not harm others, that is not its purpose. The Guardian "guards the walls" of your emotional castle and protects you from mistreatment or abuse. The Guardian is not strong in children, which is why they need our protection.

When I work with sexually abused people, a pivotal step in the healing is to help them tap into the self protective rage that is buried inside them—a physical and emotional fury that will not allow harm to happen without a deadly fight. People who have access to their inner rage are awe-inspiring. They have never breathed so deeply, yelled so loudly, focused so clearly. Once this capacity has been awakened, I know they will be vastly less likely to be harmed or exploited again. Only when the Guardian is mobilized, can a man or woman begin to establish close relationships. In fact, only then can life really proceed. A woman will feel more able and willing to bear a child, as she knows she has the capacity to protect it. (I have known fertility problems to disappear through this work—as if a woman's body would not bear a child until her mind knew it could keep it safe.)

For a marriage to thrive, both partners need to bring their Guardians along for the ride. It's not that the other person wishes them harm, just that people getting close will inevitably overstep the other's boundaries and need to be reminded. Often it's enough to say, "Hey, you are crowding me," "Don't make my mind up for me," or "Let me choose my own sweater!" Sometimes things get heated. Sometimes no amount of gentle talk is enough to root out fixed attitudes or longer term misunderstandings, and pull them into the light of day.

We made a mistake in our Fifties culture when we pursued the harmonious, sweet, and loving ideal of marriage. The passionate, heated European-style marriage has more going for it. Jung said, "American marriages are the saddest in the whole world, because the man does all his fighting at the office."

The trick is to fight consciously, carefully. You can be passionate and still choose your words carefully. So often though, when men and women are fighting nose to nose, the man doesn't actually know what he wants. All he wants is for the fighting to stop, he may say he "doesn't like fighting." But if he doesn't stay in this furnace, how can the pair ever burn off the misunderstanding and create something new and better? Perhaps the man never saw his parents fight productively. Or perhaps they were vicious, out of control, and he wants none of that. He takes every word of complaint or criticism as a spear to the heart, when from her point of view, she's just throwing mud pies. A man will collapse, or he will go off and sulk, when what is needed is to just stand there, listen, and if you see it differently say so. There is a middle way through all this.

PASSION NEEDS RULES

It's paradoxical that we can only let our feelings flow freely, and only be truly passionate, when we have certain boundaries laid down. Trust has to be there. By limits, we mean:

- Never being physical or even threatening to hit or harm.

- Never walking out of the house mid-fight (though you can walk out of the room—see below).

- Not using put-down language. No name calling, no disrespect, no sarcasm (these are often women's weapons, and she must be strong in relinquishing them).

- Staying on the point and not bringing in other material.

- Listening to the other's point of view while honoring your own.

- Taking time out, by agreement, if it becomes too heated—to think it over—and returning to continue the argument. (This latter is especially important if you feel you might become violent or irrational. The early warning signs are not hard to spot. Just say—I need to cool off right now, this is too heated for me. And go to another room.)

These rules allow you to debate cleanly and respectfully, until understanding is reached.

FIGHTING IN MARRIAGE

Fighting in marriage can be a source of great learning and growth. Marie-Louise von Franz tells a story about a friend who had a series of marriages that were extremely turbulent and painful. They always started well, but in each marriage the arguing eventually lead to physical fighting and then to divorce.

The friend's fourth husband was different. The very first time the wife "threw a fit" (her words) and began to be wildly abusive, the man simply walked quietly to his room and began packing his things. He refused to fight "dirty" as was being expected. His words are beautiful:

I know I am supposed to act like a man now and shout and hit you, but I am not that sort of man. I will not allow anyone to talk to me in the way you have, *and I am leaving.*

The woman was so shocked that she apologized. The couple are still together. It's important to point out that if the woman in this story had been making a point, asking for a change, then the man needed to stay put and listen. But this was quite different. She was "having a fit."

Because men and women have had huge problems over the last few centuries since industrialization, there has been a great legacy of abuse, betrayal, and hurt. It's possible that we can carry in us not only our own, but our mothers and fathers and grandparents accumulated rage and sorrow, and simply drop into a blind and unthinking rage which does huge harm to our ability ever to trust again. Two friends of mine, both health professionals, have a loving relationship and a strong religious commitment to their marriage. Yet both are deeply frightened on the inside because of their childhood histories of violence and mistrust. At times when they disagree, neither seems able to stop descending into massive escalation of screaming, threats, often physical blows, and one or both taking their things and driving off into the night. It's horrific for them, and for their young children, who listen to all of this from the bedroom and wonder if someone is going to get killed.

What can you do to end a pattern like this? Recognize the early warning signs. Learn to calm yourself, through deliberate strategies of breathing, meditation, slowing down when you notice you are getting overloaded. Make a commitment to govern your own words and actions. Get into a program that heals old fears and releases the nightmares of childhood, so they don't keep flashing into your present.

BEING CLOSE BUT DIFFERENT

Learning to disagree is what gets you beyond the stage of honeymoon, where, let's face it, you are essentially in love with fantasy you paint onto your partner like a convenient canvas.

Sam Keen puts it well: "Romance is all 'yes' and heavy breathing—an affair built around the illusion of unbroken affirmation. Marriage is 'yes' and 'no' and 'maybe'—a relationship of trust that is steeped in the primal ambivalence of love and hate."

"Love and hate" doesn't have to be all that dramatic. It's as simple as the switching between "I just want to lie with you here forever" and "Will you, for Chrissake, leave my desk as it is—I know where to find things!"

"But I was just cleaning it up."

"Well, *don't!*"

We all want to be close, but no one likes the feeling of being swamped. What therapists call "individuation"—becoming your own person, while staying invested and caring to each other—is a lifelong process.

GIVING UP VIOLENCE

So far, everything we have said about the genders is true of both equally. But men and women are unequal in one important way. Usually men are bigger and stronger than their partners. And neurologically, it's been found that males react to emotion more quickly and more strongly. Learning to drive a male body safely requires extra and different training than learning to be a woman.

Every community needs to have training programs for men (and sometimes for women) who wish to eliminate violence from their family situation. Here is a typical account of such a group.

In a room at a community health center, a group meets for eight weeks. There are two leaders and eight men, all of whom are there because of a history, or a fear, of violence against wives and children. As we join them, one of the leaders is talking with a man in the group who looks awkward, his arms crossed tightly across his chest.

"Dave, you say you 'roughed her up.' What does 'roughed her up' mean?"

"I pushed her around a little, nothing bad."

"How did you push her?"

"With my hand. She was swearing at me. She'd been late home from her class."

"How hard did you push her?"

"Not very hard. She just fell back against the wall and she started to cry."

"Did she look scared?"

"Yes."

"So you pushed her hard enough to make her feel pretty scared of you."

"Yes."

"How do you feel that you made the woman you love so scared?"

"Not good."

"Is that something you'd like to learn to handle better—that kind of situation?"

"Yes. That's why I'm here."

"Okay."

The process, as you can see even from this small exchange, is one of becoming more honest. If you can tell the truth to yourself, what once "just happened" becomes "a choice I made." By providing support for the difficulty of a man's life, understanding from others who have been there, and a complete unwillingness to allow bullshit, such programs gradually give a man an ability to be in absolute control of himself. It's a great feeling.

In a marriage both partners have their own methods of asserting power and control. Lacking his partner's skills in using words, feeling powerless in the bigger world (unemployed, having low status or stress at work), having a history of witnessing violence as a child, a man may default to violence more easily. However, for the pattern to be broken, men must commit themselves to giving up violence as a method. Few men have the psychopathic wish to harm and dominate—and these men are not too hard to identify. Most violent men are caught in a cycle, desperate to break out if there is an option, and have partners who love them and do not wish to leave them.

Men's groups need to be lead by men who have acknowledged and faced their own capacity for violence. They know the pressures a man feels in his life, and also the cop-outs and self-justifications.

Isolation also plays a large part in the problem. Many men in such groups state that before coming to the program they have never had friends who could listen to their situations. The men they meet in the groups are, paradoxically, more confronting and more supportive than any they have met. With this kind of male friendship, they are less dependent emotionally on their wives, so there is a new relaxation and ease in their relationships. This is close to the heart of what men's liberation is all about.

MEN CHANGING MEN

When men build new community with each other, they can reinforce new sets of rules. "It's wrong to hit women. It's wrong to hit or be sexual with children. We are your friends and that is why we tell you this. And if need be we will stop you, with legal means, if you refuse to stop yourself."

Brotherhood of this kind means other things too. For instance, not sleeping with another man's wife. Because you can understand how he would feel, and you don't want to do that. If a young woman approaches you at a bar—and tells you her husband is no good or doesn't understand her, then you tell her she needs to go and talk it through with him. It won't help to tell *you* about it!

Which brings us around to sex.

SEX AND THE CHASE
A story . . .

Many years ago, when I knew more than I do now, I occasionally ran weekend workshops for couples. One such weekend was with married couples from a church congregation:

They are all nice people. In fact, a little too nice—especially the men. Good-hearted but just too agreeable. The soft slippers, neat garden, never-a-cross-word type of guy.

We are working through a list of topics and it's Sunday afternoon, getting late. One of the topics on the list is "Sexuality and the Chase." We haven't got to this topic yet. A man in his late thirties, sitting in a beanbag, leaning comfortably against his sparky young wife, asks, "When are we going to do sexuality?"

"Oh," I say, with a grin, "we might get around to it in a little while!" (I'm teasing him, but I don't know why.) "It depends if there's enough time."

"Oh, okay," he says, and slumps back in his beanbag. My sense of mischief grows.

"Is this what he does in bed?" I ask his wife, grinning.

"Yes, it is!" she says.

She seems to know what I mean. He looks bewildered, so I elaborate.

"Well, you wanted to do something about sex. I wasn't sure. So you quit. You gave up. Don't you know you're supposed to persist? You want it handed to you on a plate?" He starts to blush, but he's not unhappy. He's catching on fast.

"You see, that's how sex works," I go on making it all up as I go along, "You need to be considerate and patient, sure, but you don't give up. You have a part of you that is wild and free and just wants to go for it!" (I want to use stronger language but it's a church group!)

"The thing you don't realize is that, treated properly, at the right time, that is what she wants too." (I have to stop speaking at that point, because his wife, out of his range of view just beside him, is biting her lip and nodding *Yes!*)

Again, poet Robert Bly has put this beautifully: "One intense sexual storm in a hay-barn means more to her than three years of tepid lovemaking. She wants passion and purpose in a man, and she carries a weighty desire in her, a passion somewhere between erotic feeling and religious intensity."

PERSIST

The secret of being a suitor (which is still needed even when you have been married for half a century), is to persist, without being a pest. Even if it takes weeks. Biology made women slow to burn (at least, some of the time) and men quick to explode. A skillful lover needs to damp down his fire but not let it go out. Foreplay and pursuit take place over days. Even when lovemaking has started in earnest, he holds back. Gradually, as tenderness, skill, and intensity of connection set her alight, he can abandon himself more and more to his passion, catching up with her in joyous abandon. A woman friend of mine expressed it this way—"It's power harnessed that I love, power driven and directed and held in just the right amount of check. That's the sexiest thing there is."

CONFIDENCE

Lovemaking and courtship take more than a little confidence on the man's part. As Marvin Allen said, "Between first meeting a gal and getting where you want to be, there are 573 chances of rejection!" In our culture we start relationships too soon or perhaps we hold back the initiation into manhood too long. A century ago you were a man at fourteen, and expected to prove it. Today we can be a boy at thirty. This does not make for good relationships with the confident and self-aware young women of today.

As boys, we can easily lose our sense of self in the heady perfume of our girlfriend's radiance. We can tumble head over heels into an inviting cleavage, and never find our way out. (As an eighteen year old, I spent Saturdays helping wash the poodle of a particularly appealing girl. It's not an interest I have really cultivated ever since!)

Older cultures forbade courtship until a boy had passed through significant initiation processes, and was man enough to keep his sense of self. This was for the boy's own good, as much as anything. Today, if you've come through some hardships in your life, achieved some worthwhile goals, made and kept good friends, been of value to others, if you know your limitations and your strengths, then you come to a woman with fascination but also with self respect—on equal terms. You are much more likely to choose well, and to find someone who wants to be a team player, rather than lead you around by your necktie. Strength attracts strength.

A SPACE OF YOUR OWN

Many men have no space of their own in the house—clearly from the decor and furnishings, the bedroom is usually the woman's space. If a man goes to work, and deals all day with pressures, and then comes home to more pressures, there isn't anywhere that he can just be. Along with having a room of one's own, goes time of one's own. Setting aside time each day to be yourself and do your thinking means you have a more equal footing in the household and less need to stay too long at the office or the bar.

Use your space to gain a sense of self. Early in the morning, or before bed, take time to find yourself again. Move in a rhythm, out and in again, mix it with the children, with visitors, with your partner.

Also use space to be with your partner. Go round the corner with her to a restaurant or park, so you can also have couple time. Use the physical world—beaches, forests, the busyness of downtown—to express the different states of mind that you want to encompass—the different aspects of yourself.

GETTING THROUGH THE LONG, DARK NIGHT

Most contemporary men get together with a woman first and then grow up second—if we're lucky and she is patient! So it's likely that some crises of growth will occur, which we will have to find our way through within the relationship. There is one outstandingly common crisis, which is probably behind 90 percent of marriage break-ups (however many other reasons are cited). You could call this stage "the long dark night." It would be more edifying if it were "the long dark night of the soul," but it's really just the long dark night of the penis! Let me explain.

We fall in love mostly by good luck. It just happens. Maintaining love is often left to luck, too. Unlike those cultures where marriages are arranged, we don't realize love is a craft that takes practice. Eventually, most men and women lose the spark—they fall out of love.

The man usually denies this to himself and is happy enough as long as his partner stays sexually available. It may be that, for men, sex has a kind of sedating, reward-at-the-end-of-the-day quality (as expressed in the hugely popular song, "My Baby Takes the Morning Train" by Sheena Easton). Sex is a compensation for the treadmill quality of the rest of life—with a mortgage, young children, and retirement still decades away.

Very often though, a woman tires of routine sex. (Or with young children, or perhaps a job, she is just plain tired). The very thing that makes a man a good husband—his devotion to being a stable provider—wears out his spirit and makes him boring. Finding sex, and marriage, unrewarding, she starts to cool down. She exerts her perfect right to not make love. The man sulks, suffers, grouches, and schemes, to no avail.

For a man with inner resources, this is a temporary setback. He admits in the first place that sex *was* actually routine, that the relationship had gone hollow—and perhaps he was not as content as he had been telling himself. He begins the concerted work to get things restarted: planning vacations or weekends together; relieving her of the pressures of children; cutting back his work commitments so as to be more energetic and interesting at home; and stopping being such a slob. Even larger changes of lifestyle are possible. There are plenty of avenues.

For men who lack inner security, however, the loss of sexual contact is devastating—far beyond its actual meaning. The average man—shut down to his feelings since childhood, numb and tense in his body—*only really feels alive when he is having sex.* Sex is the only opening to his inner body. Now this avenue is lost, too!

The problem may go deeper still. Lacking adequate fathering, he has never really unbonded from his mother. He has simply transferred his mother-needs onto his wife. So as well as a loss of *sex*, he experiences a loss of *love* at an infantile level. It's as if he's been left in his crib to starve. Many men in their late thirties and early forties have encountered this despair. The drowned school teacher at the beginning of this book was an instance of this. The depression that arises is so complete, all previous enjoyments and reasons for living seem to have turned to ashes.

The man in this position usually acts in a weak and helpless way. This just makes him even less appealing to his wife, however much she may sympathize. (She would do him no favor by relenting.) Or he may get nasty, become violent, hide money, or begin having an affair. This is almost always a serious mistake. With the new woman, he will simply replay the pattern. (Five years down the track, he will be at the same place. He finds himself, at forty-five, walking the boards with another sleepless baby, thinking, I've been here before!)

Listen carefully here. It isn't *a woman* you need at this time in your life. This whole catastrophe of the long dark night of the penis is the result of a totally mistaken belief on the part of the man *that you can't live without a woman's love.* The remedy—vitally important since we are talking about half of all U.S. marriages here—is for other men to step in and give emotional support.

This is not the same as getting you drunk. Good friends at these times will listen to you talk about your problems but also have fun, take you fishing, eat, cook, and play. They will also, when the time is right, point out that it's time you got back to your family and sorted things out. It's as if male friends and elders bathe your wounds, remind you that life is good, give you a hug, and then throw you back into the ring!

Choose your friends carefully. Some friends are on the side of your marriage and your happiness. However, a whole other group of men are losers with women and are glad to see you having problems too. They don't *want* you to stay married. Women-hating men can be found in every bar in every city of the world. Avoid them.

THE MAN WHO HAS MADE IT THROUGH

For the man who makes it through the long dark night, the rewards are great. He loses the baby-like quality of most men, and becomes more straight-backed and fierce-eyed. He is no longer in any hurry. He is very different around women—more companionable, humorous, direct. He is no longer "mother-bound" or sleazy. Comfortable in his aloneness, he approaches women as equals. Since he offers a woman real friendship and not a big empty barrel for them to fill, he is much more attractive. There's sweet irony here that when you can "take it or leave it," when love and affection are no longer a matter of life and death, then it all comes to you!

IN CONCLUSION

There will always be tension in male-female relationships— adult love isn't meant to have the same sugary-sweet harmony of a mother and baby. When an adult man and woman meet, expect sparks. Learning to dance with this tension, to use it and enjoy it as a way of defining and refining your own identity, sharing in the making of a home, raising kids, finding your place in the community and world, men and women can give each other enormous joy, and only a dash or two of grief.

IN A NUTSHELL

• Don't agree with your wife for the sake of peace. Say what is true for you. You have to walk a line—not giving in out of weakness and not bullying either. Both are signs of unnecessary fear.

• Men are less skilled in verbal debate, being given less training as boys. But you are the expert on you. Hang in there, keep talking, till you get the knack.

• Decide now never to use violence against a woman or a child. If you have trouble with this, join a men's program which addresses this problem.

• In sex and loving, much of the time the man has to make the effort. This is a matter of biology. Learn to be persistent and courtly. Be protective. Don't crowd her. Work to win her over. If sometimes you don't succeed, don't take it personally.

• Most marriages go through phases of sexual distance or shutting down. Don't mistake this for not being lovable. At the same time, don't depress yourself and just tolerate an unhappy sex life. Work to find out what is wrong, and fix it. Spend time with male friends and broaden your life. Love returns more quickly if you don't need it. Your partner is not your mother.

OTHER VOICES
The Hazards of Being Male

Something awful happens to many men after they get married. As a sensitive and aware married woman I interviewed described the married men in her neighborhood: "They're all so passive. They have to hate their wives because those guys are hardly even people. A typical weekend day for them seems to mean trimming hedges, mowing the lawns and puttering with their cars." Furthermore many married men seem to become progressively more childlike, dependent and helpless in their interactions with their wives. Wives discussing their husbands with me in private often make comments such as, "He acts like a baby," "He's become so dependent on me it scares me. He won't do anything for himself," "He acts as if he's totally helpless," and "He's always hanging around the house and getting in the way. I wish he had some more friends."

Many of these men ask their wives for permission whenever they want to do things on their own. When they describe the positive aspects of their marriage relationship it often sounds something like, "She lets me do a lot of things on my own and doesn't stay on my back, like a lot of other wives that I know." In essence, the wife has been given the role of permission-giver or mother-figure by the male.

Progressively, the married man begins to distrust his own judgment and taste. He starts to believe that he is an unaesthetic clod who is only good in the business or working world and that his taste does not measure up to hers. Like mother, she knows best. As one real-estate person expressed it to me, "I never sell to the husband. I always sell to the wife. If he likes the house, it doesn't mean anything. But if she likes it, I've got a sale."

Because he is caught in a relationship that may not be intrinsically satisfying to him, although he is not always in conscious touch with his anger, resentment and desire for autonomy, his negative feelings continually emerge indirectly in the form of passive aggression. He is "in" the relationship but not "of" it. The passive expression of his frustration and discontent assumes many forms:

1 Extreme moodiness and occasional outbursts of rage that are precipitated by relatively minor things such as a misplaced sock, laundry done late, a button that hasn't been sewn on, a toy left on the floor or a late meal.

2 Grabbing for the mail, a drink, and then hiding behind the newspaper or in front of a television set almost immediately after coming home from work.

3 Increasing expression of his wanting to be "left alone" when he's at home.

4 Increasing complaints of fatigue and physical ailments such as backaches, stomach aches and headaches.

5 A drifting of attention when his wife is speaking to him causing him to ask her frequently to repeat herself, an indication that his mind is wandering and that he is not concentrating.

6 Having to be reminded constantly about the same things which he continually seems to forget, such as hanging up his clothes, taking out the garbage, etc.

7 *A general resistance to talking about his day when he comes home in the evening.*

8 *Avoidance of sexual intimacy manifested indirectly by either coming to bed after she's fallen asleep, or falling asleep before she's come to bed. Other manifestations include bringing home work from the office, and doing it into the night, and staying up late to read or watch television.*

9 *An avoidance of eye contact with his wife.*

10 *An increasing tendency to confine his social life with his wife to activities such as going out to eat or to a movie, which do not require active interaction between them.*

11 *Generalized feelings of boredom. The boredom often disguises an impulse or desire to do things or be places other than where he is. Since he is unable to own up to his real needs, he does nothing and sits home bored instead.*

Unable to assert himself openly or to own up to his discomfort, his hidden resentment emerges in a myriad of underground ways. The message he is transmitting indirectly to his wife is "I'm afraid to do what I really want to do, or express how I really feel, so I'll avoid feeling guilty by staying at home. But you aren't going to get any satisfaction from my presence either."

—Herb Goldberg

7 Being a Real Father

WHAT DOES FATHERING mean? Listen to the language we use every day and it will tell you a lot. If we talk of "mothering" children, we get a picture of caring, nurturing, and spending long hours in close, sensitive contact. The word "fathering" means something quite different. You can "father" a child in two minutes (in the backseat of a Dodge)! At its most extreme, a father is just a sperm donor. Nothing more. Many people today see no problem with single women, or lesbian couples, seeking donor insemination, leaving fathers out completely. However, fathering is much more than this. It's an essential part of raising children of either sex. Yet the art of fatherhood has almost been lost from our homes and communities.

John Embling is a worker with kids in inner-city Melbourne. His books include *Tom—A Child's Life Regained* and *Fragmented Lives*. John works to pull kids back from homelessness, violence, and imprisonment. Here are his thoughts on fathers:

> *I spend most of my life with children, young adults, mothers—but where are the fathers? I have known only four or five fathers-as-parents, as providers, as role models, over those ten years. I have seen so many young children who need men in their home lives, men who are capable of psychologically meeting their needs.*

> Even the strongest, most capable single parent finds it difficult
> to give his or her child all that is needed to make a human
> being. But what about the single, deserted, penniless mother
> on the top floor of the Kensington Housing Commission flats.
> Where do her children look for relationships with father figures?
>   I often look around for the fathers in the lives of our children.
> I feel a sense of profound loss, of defeat, of inhumanity, as I
> see men devoid of personal contact with their children. Their
> loss, the loss of something central to human process, is also
> our loss. Something is being crippled, and all the money, tech-
> nology, bureaucracy, professionalism, ideology in the world
> won't make it right again.
>
> —John Embling, *Fragmented Lives*

The role of father has sunk to a very low point. Are fathers
necessary? One feminist writer once said, "A world without
men would be a world full of fat, happy women!" To which
we'd add, " . . . and very screwed-up children." In this chapter
we will argue that both boys and girls need fathers for specific
reasons in their development—reasons that cannot be fulfilled
by mothers on their own. Even more importantly, we believe
that boys who do not get active
fathering—either by their own
father or someone willing to step
in—will never get their lives as
men to work. It's as simple and as
absolute as that.

Something is being
crippled, and all the . . .
technology in the
world won't make it
right again

Let's assume you are a father or
plan to be one. You have love and
good intentions. But still you may be operating in a virtual
vacuum. Many of the elements you wish to bring to par-
enting your children—consistency, firmness, warmth, and
involvement—you may have never received from a male

figure yourself. You want to pass on the message of healthy masculinity to your children, even though you have never received it yourself. The software has been lost. There is a problem in turning your love into action.

Fathers today are highly motivated, even desperate, to "get it right" because they feel so acutely that their own child-hoods were inadequate and painful. Many men's groups spend much of their time sharing ideas and helping each other to be better dads. Some groups have also begun to help each other with their children ("uncling," if you like). They may organize day trips, camping expeditions, and so forth, creating more opportunities for their children to know good men and experience the variety and richness of men of different ages. What we once had as our birthright there in our villages a hundred years or ten thousand years ago, is being recreated.

DROPPING THE OLD ROLES

The first step to being a good dad is to shed some of the old and toxic role models. These were often limiting and impoverished, and yet sit heavily like old videotape collections in our head. Unless we get rid of these "tapes," all it takes is someone to accidentally hit the play button, and we will suffer them all over again—speaking and behaving to our children the way our fathers spoke and acted toward us.

Author John Lee describes four kinds of defective father that predominated in years past. Here they are, loosely summarized . . .

The man who would be king

This was the man who, having (presumably) worked hard all day, returned home to be waited on by his loyal wife-servant and seen-but-not-heard children. He was king of the house and ruled his castle kingdom from his recliner. His family tiptoed around him, careful not to "bother" him. The only time this father got really involved was to dish out punishments or pardons. This was also the "wait until your father gets home" father.

> *My dad had an over-developed attachment to his roof. He talked about his roof a lot, and referred to it constantly when I dared question the King's decree for me. "This is my house. You live under my roof. As long as you are under my roof you'll do as you're told. When you get your own roof you can do whatever you want to, but while you're under my roof you'll do what I say when I say it." "Damn," I thought to myself. "I can't wait to get my own roof."—John Lee, At My Father's Wedding*

The critical father

Full of put-downs and nit-picking, driven by his own frustration and anger. This father was certainly active in the family, but in totally negative, frightening ways. "Is that the best you can do?" "Can't you get anything right?" "You stupid idiot, look what you've done!" Whatever was frustrating him—his job, his own father, his lack of success in life, even his unexpressed love for his children—was turned into an acid which ate away at his children's well-being.

The passive father

This guy gave up all duties, responsibilities, and power to his wife, the mother. Backing down also to the kids, his boss, relatives, society, the government, and so on. Homer Simpson is this kind of dad most of the time. He lost his backbone, if he ever had one, somewhere, way back, and now it's all just too hard to even think about. Apart from an occasional sarcastic comment or half-hearted complaint, he was never really there. Unable to stand the heat, he would retreat into a newspaper, TV, alcohol, or his garden shed. His kids grew up hating him for what he wasn't.

The absent father

This man might have been a capable, even powerful man, but not in the family arena. He was off having a career, leaving early and returning late at night. When he made love to your mother to create you, he was thinking about something else! He wasn't at your sports events or your school concert. He might have paid for all kinds of goodies for you and even been polite and kindly if you chanced to meet him in the hallway one night. But he wasn't any use to you as a father because a father has to be there.

These days it seems almost too much to ask—a father who is active and involved, happily part of the family, a father who is his own man, and also is willing to be a partner to his wife and a friend and teacher to his kids.

It's not so hard, if you are willing to learn as you go along. Those of us who had good fathers remember all the little things—playing with us when we were small, taking us to school, buying shoes or a jacket, playing in the yard, going to sports days, setting rules, deciding on what happens when those rules are broken, bathing us, tending us when we were sick. We remember the kindness and patience, the givingness of it all, which we simply took for granted, but now are in awe to think of. The passive man, the absent man, the superior man, leaves all these to someone else. And he misses all the small delights that happen along the way.

HOW MEN AND BOYS WERE SPLIT

For hundreds of thousands of years the human race lived in small nomadic groups of at most thirty people. Perhaps in your whole life, if you had lived in those times, you would meet only two hundred people. Even when the New Stone Age ended and recorded history began, for four thousand years we lived only in villages and very small towns.

In the timeless rhythm of village and tribal life, men were deeply a part of the raising of children. You still see this today in the third world—men carrying the toddlers to the fields on their shoulders, sons and nephews learning from the older men all day and every day. Along with the skills of hunting and making things, boys were learning how to be a man. It was a long apprenticeship. Forty-year-olds were still learning. Old men and women led the community by virtue of their vast knowledge and experience. All day, every day, boys drank in the tone, style, and manner of being a man from a dozen or so available role models, who were tough but also tender with them as needed.

Surprisingly to most of us, it's now thought by anthropologists that life in hunter-gatherer times was relatively easy, even leisurely. Knowing hundreds of useful plants, and the ways of animals, food gatherers relied on skill more than sheer exertion. The desert aboriginal people in my part of the world (a very harsh environment) could meet their food and shelter needs with only a couple of hours' effort per day. (We've clearly gone backwards). Certainly in our prehistory there was famine, disease, warfare, but these were interruptions in a timeless pattern of relative plenty. If there was a weak link, it was the absolute dependency on each new generation becoming skilled, safe, integrated members of the community. Nothing consumed as much time and energy as the training and socialization of the young. And so they did it well.

Then, suddenly, in an unprecedented way (in the ecological blink of an eye), it all began to change. The shift to agriculture, the birth of cities, and then, just one hundred and fifty years ago, the Industrial Revolution arrived and changed everything. In the British Isles, for instance, villagers were driven from their homes in millions to free up the land for wool, which was more profitable than crops and took much less labor. Villages were razed to the ground by the landlords' hired men, so the people could never return. Men away at wars returned to find their homes gone, their families sometimes starved to death. The towns needed a workforce—factory workers, miners, and laborers. It was a matter of change or die. (The same pattern is still taking place all across Asia and Africa today.)

In the new industrial era, fathers, for the first time in history, worked away from their sons and daughters, waking before first light and returning after dark, six and sometimes seven days a week. When fathers came home they were exhausted, angry, defeated men. The children learned to avoid them. For the first time in human history, a generation of boys grew up without being fathered in the true sense. Today we take this arrangement for granted. Fathers work, mothers raise children (or put them in day care for other women to raise). Female school teachers civilize our boys. Boys have a choice: to comply and be good little boys or else misbehave. The "misbehavers" form gangs for solace and self-protection, looking for the masculine energy they do not realize they are missing.

> When asked about the father doll, they replied, "He's at work."

FATHER-ABSENCE TODAY

From a son's point of view, little has changed for one hundred and fifty years. Now fathers work in cleaner, safer environments—but the effect on the family is the same. It could even be worse. A man who takes up desk work in an office has little in common with his son and often cannot even explain to his son what he is doing. Daddy "goes to work," where he simply disappears into incomprehensible activity, for nine or ten hours a day.

In the mid-1970s the Mattel toy company wanted to market a family of dolls called "The Heart Family." First they trialed the sets, which comprised (naturally!) a mother, father, and two children. The test children, in numerous samples, took the father doll and set him aside. Then they played with the mother and children. When asked, "What about the father doll?" they replied, "He's at work." Father's work had no substance or meaning to these children, and he was rarely used in the make-believe play. (Eventually, of course, the problem was solved. The father dolls were sold separately with big muscles, armor, and a gun!)

When a father is only around for an hour or two at night, the mother's values and style become the values and style of the house. Dad is a kind of visitor, a shadowy figure. Something is missing. For boys, there is no experience of maleness in action. What children get from a career father is not his energy, nor his teaching, nor his substance, but only his mood. And at seven o'clock at night, that mood is mostly irritation and fatigue.

For girls it's different—they can learn to be a woman from Mom and her friends—but the boys cannot learn to be a man. Immersed in the talk of women, a girl would grow into an articulate and self aware woman. The boy would have to make up his masculinity from imagination, the movies, and his friends.

A spectrum of experiences characterized twentieth century families. Some men managed in spite of everything to be a strong and loving presence in their family. One man told me "Dad was away all week, he was a salesman. But on Saturdays he would tell mom to stay in bed or go out with her friends, and he would cook for us, play with us, take us swimming in the summer. Saturdays were dad days, and they were heaven." On the other extreme, almost half of marriages collapsed under the strain, and many children grew up with no man at all in the home. (One shocking study claimed that after a year of divorce, a third of men no longer saw their children at all.)

THE GANG AS A SUBSTITUTE DAD

In communities where fathers are mostly absent—whether affluent or poor—the phenomenon of the teenage gang can be found. As mid-adolescence arrives, boys hunger for some outward movement into the world of men; this need is so strong they will follow anyone—and a seventeen-year-old can be perceived as a father substitute by a lonely fourteen-year-old. Yet the seventeen-year-old has no wisdom to impart, and is not in charge of his own impulses, let alone those of others. Disaster stalks close at hand. Teenage gangs do not occur in communities where the different ages interact and care for each other—they are a symptom of a community in trouble. The gang members' behavior (which they themselves do not consciously understand) is clearly designed to provoke older adult males into taking notice of them. Small town policemen who know their jobs are fully aware of this—they are acting as the community's surrogate dad, and it's the kids without dads that give them all their grief.

Parents worry about peer group pressure leading their child into drugs, sex or crime. They should take note that the greatest predictor of peer group problems is a poor relationship with *the same sex parent*. (For girls it's the mother-daughter relationship, for boys the father-son.) A teenage boy who enjoys the company and involvement of his father and his father's friends does not need to look toward an eighteen-year-old gang leader for leadership. These boys will be still be part of a peer group, but they have the inner strength to hold back from any stupidities the group may wander into, and in fact they will exercise leadership naturally as a result of their healthy linkage back to more mature maleness.

CONFIDENT MALENESS

Even in intact families, where fathers care and want to do their best, the demands of the workplace mitigate against success. It's highly likely that boys have a biological need for several hours of one-to-one male contact per day. To have a demanding job, commute to work in a city, and raise sons well is extremely hard. Something has to give.

It gets worse still. A number of psychoanalysts and family therapists around the world have noted that father-absence creates some special side effects. It isn't just that the absent father is a neutral persona. You can't be neutral in a family. Occupants of the same household can only love or hate each other. A son either loves or hates his father—it's rarely an indifferent relationship. Having something you deeply need, so near and yet so far, produces a great intensity of feeling.

The modern career dad has these problems to contend with. Men in the past showed their love by working hard and long. The father as a walking wallet. But sadly, we do not get appreciated for it since it is our presence, not our bounty that is hungered for by our children. (Of course they want our bounty too!—Kids still ask for the computer game or other toys, but with enough father-time they soon forget these substitutes.)

Women need to be very clear about what they ask of their husbands—since men are likely, by default, to assume that it is their earning capacity that is their biggest contribution. A friend of ours, a bank manager, married a woman who once mentioned during the courtship that she would never have married a poor man. He became a compulsive gambler to keep up the impression of success. This led to him embezzling from his bank and a prison sentence. She left him for another man. It was a tough lesson.

The Fifties father was strong and silent. But what use is that to a growing boy? He needs to know the words, the feelings, the values. He needs a man who will share enough of his inner world for him to begin to form his own. And he needs to see a man acting from his values—to learn how relationships work. One man told me "My parents never argued or fought in front of us kids. They went into the bedroom, and you couldn't hear what was being said. When it came to fighting in my own marriage, I didn't know how to do it. My wife wondered why I was asking her to come to the bedroom!"

All through the twentieth century, girls grew up with women around them all day, every day. They soaked in the example of many competent, varied, and expressive women. By the time they were adults, their femaleness was rich and broadly based. Boys, however, got so little male contact, that their masculinity was a thin, wavy line. How could they feel anything other than insecure? In arguments, in discussions at work or home, they were lost. "She puts her case so well. Her words are well chosen. All her friends agree!" But how can he articulate himself? What has he to draw on? Faced with this, a man may cave in, or run away, or worst of all hit out. In counseling, I invariably encounter men who simply cannot be honest with their partners. It's not that they lie, but that they cannot find the truth—their truth. They cannot formulate a self, yet a self is needed before you make a relationship. It leads to enormous grief. Without confidence to put your case, nothing can be resolved. And confidence, for a man, depends on extensive contact with healthy and diverse kinds of older men. Father hunger rages like a famine across the land.

GETTING IT RIGHT

What can a man do? For a start, show up in your own children's lives! Begin during pregnancy; if your unborn baby hears your voice often, they will turn to face you once they are born, recognizing that familiar rumble.

When your baby is small, hold him against you often and he will also feel your voice. A man's voice resonates deep in his chest and vibrates through a held baby, in a way he will come to love.

When you take him into your arms at the moment of his birth, have your shirt open. Do not use soap, deodorant, or scented cosmetics of any kind, so that your child bonds to the natural, clean, sweaty smell of you. Your unique odor signature will become reassuring to them. Don't be separated from your wife and child in the hospital. Sleep in the room, care for the child so your wife can get some sleep. Of course, respect her wish to have time with the child alone too. Do not let nurses take your child to a nursery, when it can have its parents' own care. Arrange some time off work for at least a month, or three months if you can, so that the early days can be unhurried. Teach yourself to cook!

Watch for competitive feelings. On the cover of *Families and How to Survive Them* (John Cleese and Robyn Skinner's best-selling book), there is a cartoon of a man watching his wife breastfeed the new baby. The man is sucking a pacifier, and looking very unhappy. When a new baby arrives, watch out for, and acknowledge, competitive feelings if they arise. Your wife loves you as well as the baby. But it's natural for her to switch, hormonally, to the kind of devotion that makes her able to care for the child and love doing it, in the first year. Support her, find a few minutes a day with her just to "link up" and be patient. She'll come back to you!

BEING THERE FOR YOUR SON

The Cleese-Skinner book also includes a simple and profound cartoon in which a boy walks across a bridge, over a river, from his mother's side to his father's. The mother looks worried, the father smiles shyly. This symbolizes an essential stage in male development. Around the age of six, the primary identification of the boy seems to switch. He will love and relate intensely to his mother but he is not "hers" quite so much any more. He actively wants to be with, and be like, his father. It's not that he is leaving the mother, so much as adding the father to the picture. The boy can only do this if his father is around, available, and interested in sharing time with him. Doing things with him, good-naturedly challenging and testing him, but never wounding or belittling him. Here are some ways to do this.

PLAY-WRESTLING

If you want to get along well with boys, you have to learn to wrestle. Children of both sexes love to get down on the floor and play rough and tumble, be held in the air, be tickled, try to pin your arms down, play games of all kinds. Boys who feel secure love their fathers or other men to do this with them; they are excited by the competition of matching strength and agility, and love the closeness as well.

Several important and symbolic lessons are being learned while doing this seemingly fun activity. The first is "not hurting." Inevitably, a child wrestling on the carpet will hurt an adult by being too boisterous, not careful enough with an elbow or a knee. If this happens, the father stops the action, and says clearly to the boy "Your body is precious. My body is precious. So we need one or two rules. Like not kneeing or hitting. Can you handle that?"

The boy usually agrees. It will happen more than once, of course, and be handled the same way. The aim is to learn how to fight without harm, to use lots of strength but not hurt themselves or others. A potent lesson is being learned here. When the boy is older, he will almost always be stronger and larger than his girlfriend or wife. He must know how to debate, take criticism, experience strong emotions and, at the same time, never use his physical strength to dominate or hurt her. The restraint learned by actual wrestling will come in handy in the verbal wrestling all couples need to do from time to time. The boy learns to contain his strength from the example of a father who never hurts him and who doesn't allow him to hurt others.

WINDING UP AND WINDING DOWN

There is a unique pattern of play that fathers all over the

world seem to demonstrate. I'm grateful to Alastair Spate, who described this pattern to me as follows:

> *Imagine two parents on a living-room floor with a two-year-old boy and a pile of blocks. The mother encourages the child to play with the blocks and at least construct a pile or some sort of rough structure. Typically, at some stage, the father will transform himself into a roaring monster-cum-bulldozer, knock over the blocks and provoke peals of delight in the child. From then, the two males "wind up" in challenge and response, giggling and hooting, rivaling each other to make the biggest mess.*
>
> *When the father eventually senses some disapproval, or at least concern, in the mother, he begins to "wind down" the play until a breathless equilibrium returns to the room and the boy rests in the arms of either of the parents.*
>
> *This sort of play is very much the father's specialty. The crucial thing is the winding down. Here a father teaches his child, through play, the mastery of his energy and angers, sets the limits of aggression and how to stay in charge of one's emotions and not be flooded by them.*
>
> *Most readers will have seen the uncontrolled inner and outer rages and depressions of the under-fathered boy, whose first experience of male limit-setting is likely to be the police, truant officer, or warden in early adolescence—and by then he is literally a marked man. (Or marked and not yet a man.) He never learned through this uniquely fatherly play how to become the master in his own house of angers, dreams, yearnings, and energy.*

And you thought you were just playing! "Winding oneself down" turns out to be a vital, life-saving skill—learned on the living-room floor or the back lawn. It frees you from being overtaken by your own emotions. This is the gift a good, physically comfortable father can give.

IDENTIFYING THE UNDER-FATHERED BOY

Boys who are under-fathered can be diagnosed easily. They fall into two distinct types. One type takes on macho-mania: the wearing of aggressive clothes, collecting violent toys and comics, or (if older) carrying knives and studying weapons and war obsessively. This type will usually group in highly competitive and low-quality friendships with other neglected boys or young men.

The other type is under-confident—a "Momma's boy"—and is often depressed. Younger boys of this type often have problems with bedwetting or soiling. They tend to get picked on at school, are reluctant to try new things or go to new places, and often have irrational fears.

Both these types suffer from the same problem: father-hunger. Mothers will often not be able to fix these problems on their own. As a father, it's your job, and warmth and involvement is your toolkit.

DISCIPLINE

In the bad old days, fathers were often the discipline "bad guy," the "enforcer." The fact that they were away from the house all day made them scarier. "Wait till your father gets home!" was the last ditch threat of exhausted and desperate moms. Today, the scene is different. Wimpy fathers are everywhere. They leave discipline to their wives or, worse still, undermine them: "Let the kids be—they aren't being that bad"; "Just relax, honey, it doesn't really matter." (Such men are in for a short marriage and a terrible sex life!)

Women and children need men to be at least equal partners in discipline. Boys especially require a certain good-natured combativeness in order to get the message through. Men who are comfortable with their masculinity enjoy this matching of strengths. Often they can do it without feeling threatened and without the same sense of exhaustion that women may feel from being "hard" on children.

There is another reason why fathers need to take a tougher role. The feelings of a mother for her child are primarily tender, and the child reciprocates this. If a great deal of disciplining is being done by the mother, especially if it is negative and critical, a boy can start to feel that his mother hates him. Many mothers tell me, "Every time I open my mouth, it's to criticize." A boy can feel the mother-love eroding. If the father is playing his part though, the mother relaxes, feels supported, and can be less cold or harsh as a result.

If the father "takes on" the son—talks firmly and clearly about what is and isn't acceptable and if he reinforces this with nonviolent but firm follow-up—then the wife is able to relax and can remain more loving. If a boy sees mom and dad working together in discipline, backing each other up, he calms down more easily.

Discipline only really works when father and child already have a loving connection established—a "trust fund" of good experiences together. That's why the disciplinarian dad of old was so hated. He didn't do enough good things with you, so it was easy to believe that he was doing discipline because he hated you.

The essence of good discipline is to get engaged, eyeball to eyeball, and be definite—so that children can state their case but are also made to listen to yours. This is quite the opposite of the techniques of isolation, star charts, and mechanical means that modern psychology imposed on us. Children today do not need more remoteness. They need you to get involved.

MOTHER-SON CONFLICT

> One of the most important developmental tasks, which a boy
> must successfully accomplish in order to achieve satisfying inti-
> mate relationships with women later in life, is that of separating
> emotionally from the mother. The boy must come to experience
> himself as profoundly independent of his mother—of her emo-
> tional states, of her needs, and of her sexual identity.
>
> —Douglas Gillette in *Wingspan*

In his mid-teens, a boy needs to be able to recognize that he
can live without his mother. The better a job she has done in
nurturing and teaching him, the more vital it is that he realizes he can stand alone, and not need her. If he's to make space
in his heart to live independently, to get close to other women
of his own age, he needs to move away just a little from his
mother. If this stage goes well, he will return to her, as a
friend, with lifelong depth and warmth. If it does not, which
in modern men is often the case, their relationship will be
awkward, and he may remain strangely and compulsively
juvenile and impotent around her, and around other women,
sometimes for the rest of his life.

The father, and other men that can and should be part of
the boy's world, provide a safe anchor so that the son can distance from his mother, and yet still find the world a supportive place. The boy moves progressively out into the larger
world, by widening his circles of support.

Some of this seems to be "wired in" and explains much typical and rather disruptive behavior. Around the age of fourteen
(when hormone levels surge, and testosterone rises to about
eight times its baseline level) boys will intuitively begin to
distance from mothers. Without knowing why, they will pick
fights, act disrespectful, argue, and generally make themselves

unattractive. A cave-man type of scene often occurs where the boy may be rude or aggressive to his mother over some small matter. The father, hearing this going on, will stride in and use those time honored words "Don't speak to your mother like that." The message is twofold—to the woman, that she has an ally and need never feel intimidated in her own home. And to the boy—that these adults are aligned as a team, and committed to him growing up well.

This isn't to imply that his wife can't take care of herself, only that she doesn't have to do it alone. This scene, which many of us remember, is a sign that everything is on track. A lone mother must manage this time with great care, as without any help, it can so easily slide into yelling or hitting, an impossible situation for mother and son. She must deflect things by saying something like this. . . . "We're both too emotional right now. Let's leave it for a couple of hours, and talk about it when we've cooled down." Later she can talk with her son about the need for them both to get along, and have some basic rules of respect. (In extreme cases, she may have to make this a rule of the boy being able to stay living in the home—but it's better if both parties can agree as equals that they won't be disrespectful.) A mother will need a great deal of humor and support from friends at this stage. A grandfather, uncle, or man friend who can talk with the boy at this age, pointing out the need for respecting his mother, is priceless.

A son thus makes a three step journey. From mother to father. And then there comes a time when a father is not enough either. . . .

A MENTOR FOR YOUR SON

Even the best fathers cannot raise their sons alone. Fathers need extra help from other men to do this properly. In a houseful of boisterous and defiant sons, or even with just one boy, more manpower is needed. In tribal situations the whole male community got involved with the teenage boys, mentoring, training, and initiating them. A father could count on all kinds of help, and boys could count on positive input— usually more relaxed and accepting than fathers manage to be.

A boy in his mid to late teens needs other men to step in, who will teach him skills, give him a sense of worth, and take him out beyond the family walls. In other words, he needs a mentor or two. His own father may be a mentor to someone else's son. Different from fathering, mentoring is an informing but less emotionally charged role. In the old days, the mentor, not the father, was the person who taught a boy his craft for life. This arrangement took the heat out of the father-son relationship, which can get very tense, as anyone knows who has taught their teenager to drive a car!

> A fishing club isn't really about fishing, or a baseball club about baseball . . .

In practice this means a few simple steps. If you have sons, you also need to have groups of male friends whom they can be around, so that they feel accepted into the adult male world. While a father and son will hopefully share some interests, the mentors may widen the range and prevent the son being limited to what the father can offer. There will always be deeply intellectual fathers with athletic and extrovert sons, and vice versa. This needn't be a problem if the father is willing to allow and encourage good men from among his acquaintances who can supplement what he offers and so create a balanced adolescent experience.

> *A boy needs help to learn about his own gifts and identity, and help to learn how to identify someone who has mastered the skills that are the birthright of his nature.*

> *Their lives seldom expose them to mature men doing things of such quality as to inspire a boy's emulation and his willingness to discipline himself in anticipation of being ready for his own chance later in life. In this light, we should not be surprised that our teenagers have grown apathetic about preparing for roles that are either invisible to them or that exercise no charm over their imaginations.*
>
> —John Palmour in *Wingspan*

Wise parents understand that the myriad activity groups around which people organize their leisure time serve a more important purpose. A fishing club isn't really about fishing, or a baseball league about baseball (though part of the game involves treating these things as being of extraordinary importance!). They are really just ways that men can care for each other and take boys into tutelage, give them positive messages, and so provide a vehicle for character growth and maturation. Today this is often misunderstood and the point of the activity is lost—for instance when coaches encourage cheating or violence on the field, or the use of steroids. Done well, though, these activities give our sons a tribe to belong to. They can inspire and help him find his true direction and philosophy for life.

WHAT A SINGLE MOTHER CAN DO

Single mothers I speak with are usually very alert to the need for male models for their sons. Once they find a way to meet this need, many problems of young sons—such as shyness or aggressiveness—disappear. If you are a single mother of boys, visit your sons' school and ask if they can have a male teacher next year. Choose the athletic, musical, scouting avenues that have good men in them. Be choosy. Select on the basis of, "Are these the kind of men I want my son to turn into?" Be careful—sometimes sexually abusive men prey on fatherless boys, exploiting their craving for male affection.

Men can be very helpful, if they are clear on what their job is. A mother in a ToughLove group (a self-help group for embattled parents) told how her fourteen-year-old son would simply not get out of bed and go to school in the mornings. Several men from her group offered to go, as a team, and rouse her son from bed to get him off to school each morning. They showed up in the boy's room one morning and urged him firmly but good naturedly through the morning routine. The boy was shocked but somewhat amazed that anyone cared! After a couple of visits, they only had to drop in briefly, then be "on call." The boy got his act together.

Single mothers can raise boys well, but not alone. They have to have the help of a wider network. Their self-care skills must be honed to avoid negativity or flying off the handle, yet maintain good discipline—especially around the mid-teens. "It takes a village to raise a child"—and the village needs to have both women and men.

FATHERS WITH DAUGHTERS

Daughters need some special things from fathers. One of these is affirmation. This means the feeling of being appreciated, admired but never invaded or exploited, so that they can practice conversation and mutual admiration with a "safe" male. Through talking with their fathers and other older men, daughters can gain assurance, feel worthwhile, and know they do not "need" the first boy who looks at them. Knowing how to be comfortable around men is priceless for a girl.

The quality of her mother's and father's relationship is important too. Knowing that her father aligns with her mother at a deep level, and can't be seduced or undermined, means that she recognizes boundaries. She learns how to say "no" and take "no" for an answer. If Mom and Dad get along well, she will want at least that quality of relationship in her own marriage.

Fathers of teenage daughters will naturally feel some protectiveness and jealousy. Within reason, this is useful. It doesn't hurt for boyfriends to be moderately terrified! Some clear safety limits can be set, appropriate for the daughter's age and stage. A friend of mine, who is divorced from his first wife, learned that his thirteen-year-old daughter was at a party with some people who were far beyond her depth to deal with. He quickly gathered two large male friends, and went and got her. She made a token complaint, but was basically very relieved.

Being trustworthy is something a teenager has to prove—it isn't a right. At the same time, a father has to guard against being jealous out of his own needs. He needs to envisage his daughter moving out, being strong in making her own choices, having a happy life. No one will ever be good enough for her, but luckily it isn't his choice!

Fathers are the "first man" in a girl's life. It is now believed by researchers into family dynamics, that this sets her expectations about all men, and strongly affects her choice of a mate. If her father is abusive, she may find herself attracted to abusive men. If he is distant, she will choose distant men. If her father is kind, treats her with respect, is interested in her and her views, then she will choose a mate with these qualities. Such is the awesome power—to bless or to wound—that fathers carry.

DEFENDING AND PROTECTING

To a boy, a father should represent strength and protection. For some little boys this can be life changing. One client of mine, Sean, when he was aged nine, had been at boarding school for only two weeks when the principal called him into his office, locked the door, and began to sexually abuse him.

The principal gave dire threats to the boy should he ever tell anyone. The abuse was repeated over and over again.

When Sean's father visited the school at the end of term, the principal met with him to discuss Sean's progress. Sean came into the office and immediately took in the scene. The powerful monster-principal, smug at his desk; his father, without a chair to sit on, was perched on a woodbox beside the hearth. Immediately Sean knew that his father had no power or confidence in this place. He said nothing about the sexual abuse to his father, who left oblivious. Sean remembers to this day the smile the principal gave him as his father departed. The abuse continued all that year.

Young men need protection. Robert Bly speaks angrily about the abuse of young men by the generals in Vietnam. These nineteen- and twenty-year-olds, often with idealistic or religious backgrounds, found themselves immersed in bloodshed, horror, and the ambiguity of Vietnam. Their father-figure generals and lieutenants then sent them to the brothels of Thailand to "let off steam," destroying their feeling for womanhood or tenderness and completing their disillusionment with life. Tens of thousands of these men committed suicide or retreated into drugs during or since that conflict.

At any age, men, through their isolation, can be extraordinarily vulnerable. A nurse friend of mine came across an old man crying in the stairwell of a hospital. She asked him what was wrong, and he told her that he was to have his tongue surgically cut out that day because it was cancerous. She talked with him for a time. At the end of the conversation, he had decided to cancel the surgery. He wished to live out his life— he was eighty-four—with his ability to speak and taste intact. He might die sooner, but he would die an intact human being.

SHIELDING YOUNG MEN FROM SOUL ASSAULTS

There are many assaults on the souls of men, and they begin

early. Some women hate all men and will see in male children an avenue of revenge. The son of a friend of mine went for his first day at school. He was, and is, a talkative, sparrow-like little boy—full of life. The young female teacher became angry at his chattiness, half an hour into the first school lesson of his life. She told him to stand by the wastebasket in the corner. He didn't hear her correctly—he thought she said in the wastebasket—and so that is where he stood. She let him stay there for ten minutes, occasionally ridiculing him to the class.

Unless boys are protected, how else can they keep their tender feelings intact? Unless we bring a nurturing fierceness to our lives, how can we ever heal? Men's leader Michael Meade specializes in programs bringing together men from different races, often in tense ghetto situations. He often reads pieces of poetry at these gatherings. As he reads, men begin quietly weeping. I have often seen the same thing in men's meetings and forums. It's clear that enormous amounts of baggage are being carried by boys and men, which have not found an outlet other than violence. Not for centuries have men been able to be so open. Something very good and important is beginning to happen.

PROTECTING YOUR SON'S SEXUAL DEVELOPMENT

If you have teenage sons, it's a good idea to let them close their bedroom doors and have some privacy. Don't ever barge in unannounced. Then they can relax about their experimentation with their bodies! A sensuous and accepting attitude to masturbation is needed in order for boys to learn to be relaxed lovers. The chance to read and see quality erotica—material that shows men and women in equal and enjoyable contact—will help. Never force, invade, or push sexuality on children. Simply allow their natural interest and natural sense of privacy to be there. Boys will probably obtain soft porn magazines, but these are not appropriate before the age of about sixteen, and the images shouldn't be plastered on walls! Let your sons know it's okay to admire women's bodies but always to see women as people. Much of this material is sexist, phony, and deceptive in its role-modeling. If accessed too young, boys can get fixated too much and not move comfortably to relating to real girls. A middle path can be found that affirms sexuality, but keeps some specialness around it too.

AVOIDING CHEAPNESS

In the movie *The Rose* the heroine, beautifully played by Bette Midler, is a blowsy, addicted, past-her-prime rock singer. In one critical scene, she is waiting in a recording studio along with some country musicians. She bats her eyes at a young boy in a Western shirt, who looks about seventeen, and he responds, albeit awkwardly. She is about to move into major seduction mode when the boy's father walks into the room, sees what is happening, and cuts her dead. "Don't try that cheap slut behavior with my son," he tells her (or words to that effect).

It's a jolting moment in the film, and it takes the wind out of her sails, too. Perhaps because she knows that the father is right. He is a musician too, but out of a different mold—a craftsman, clean-cut and straight-backed—and he has named a wrong. What she was doing was on one level harmless, even flattering to the young man. On another level it was inappropriate, uncaring, a female form of sexual harassment.

Boys need to understand that girls are capable of misusing them, that a penis can be a handle to get dragged around by. A female office worker in her late teens, interviewed for Bettina Arndt's courageous documentary, "When 'No' Means 'Maybe,'" illustrated this perfectly. She talked gaily about the pleasure of getting her dates sexually overheated, only to turn them down. It was a game, played for the power buzz it gave her, and she saw no reason to be ashamed.

It's not uncommon for a man to visit a prostitute just before he commits suicide. Sex, love, loneliness, and desperation can get terribly confused for men, and it's important to talk to boys about the difference between love and lust, and that sometimes people will be hurt you if you can't tell the difference.

WHAT IF YOUR SON IS GAY?

For some parents, the normal concerns about sexuality are complicated by the discovery that their son is gay. Having a homosexual son or daughter can cause pain because it bulk erases the future fantasies we all hold for our children. The question "Why?" is often a source of torment, which is really needless. The research on sexual preferences leans heavily toward the die being cast while a baby is still in the womb—and that certain hormonal switching in the brain at this time leads to a young person being gay or lesbian. Still, family dynamics may sometimes play a role. A distant father can set up the conditions for a young man to seek older men, in a way that confuses affection and sexuality. Gay clients of mine have often referred to seeking in their lover the father who never loved them. As in a straight relationship, this is bound to cause some grief.

What it all boils down to is the concerns of parents of gay teenagers are just the same as the concerns of any parent. They want their son to have a happy life. They hope that he will handle his sexuality in a responsible and self-respecting way. And they hope he will find a stable partnership if this is his wish.

Sex, whatever form it takes, is still basically a beautiful and joyful thing. Young gay people discovering their sexuality need acceptance and understanding. They also need a wider society that is not homophobic or persecutory—where healthy role-models of gay people are out in the open making good lives for themselves. It's tough enough being a teenager without being in a persecuted minority.

AFFIRMING THE SACREDNESS OF SEX

The urge to conceal details of human sexuality from children is not just based on prudishness. Perhaps it comes from a more ancient understanding—that the power of sex is not to be trivialized by passing into minds not yet able to comprehend it. There are other experiences that should come first—simple things like how to be good friends, how to respect other people, know about consequences. (The book and movie *Snow Falling On Cedars* portrayed very sensitively how disastrous a sexual relationship could be if it happens at too young an age.) The older, and more experienced, one comes into the heat of a sexual relationship, the less likely one is to be burned by it.

Sometimes a progressive Christian, Buddhist, or Islamic-based sex education succeeds far better than the secular forms, which aim to be value-free but just end up sounding mechanical. Religious views at least emphasize the joy of sex and some kind of sacred context in which it takes place. Like putting a wall around a garden, we increase the beauty by separating it from the everyday.

> In America, half of all children will spend time in a fatherless home

ABANDONED SONS ARE WAITING FOR THEIR FATHERS

Millions of American boys grow up without knowing their fathers. If you're a separated father, a father whose child was adopted, or a father who has donated sperm, the thing to remember is that somewhere your son or daughter will be waiting to know you. And know your side of the story. Not from idle curiosity—but because in some deep sense, his life's progress depends on it. Whatever you can do to be in contact and give him access to who and what you are, that will be helpful. Some separated fathers refuse to contact their children, or feel its best they don't try. I believe this is a terrible mistake. Even if it's difficult, there is hostility, and barriers are put in your way, at least find a way to let your child know you think of them, and care, and are ready to know them when they are able to come to you.

Sometimes a teenage son living with his mother will unconsciously start to make life so difficult for her that she will consider letting him go to his father to live. On occasions, to everyone's surprise, this can be just the right thing for "finishing off" a young man's development. In spite of the difficulties, there is enormous satisfaction and peace of mind if you take on your proper role here. There can be compensations in at least getting parenthood right, if not marriage. Some men have told me they only got close to their children after they divorced their wives.

FATHERLESS CHILDREN

Are you thinking of divorce? Here is some of what we know about the effect of having a father involved and in the home . . .

- Boys and girls both have greater self-esteem if their fathers are still in the home.

- They do better in school, stay in school longer, become more qualified, and are more likely to be employed.

- Children with fathers in the home are less likely to be sexually abused, less likely to have trouble with the law, and less likely to be beaten up.

- Girls are less likely to be raped or experience early sexual behavior or teenage pregnancy.

- Daughters without fathers are more "malleable" and adapted to pleasing men than are daughters who are secure in a father's love and respect.

- Boys with no fathers, or with fathers who are not around much, are much more likely to be violent, to get into trouble, to do poorly in schools, and to be a member of a teenage gang in adolescence.

- Families without a man are usually poorer, and children of these families are more likely to move down rather than up the socioeconomic ladder.

- Men who are close to their children are less likely to divorce.

- Parents who divorce tend to have kids who divorce too.

That's probably enough!

The old dilemma we were given in the past was to stay in an unhappy marriage "for the sake of the kids," or to seek our own fulfillment first and leave if a marriage wasn't working. What kids need is actually neither—they need us to be working on our marriage, committed to addressing differences, working at it right there before their eyes. Assuming it's not a fatally flawed situation—of violence, deceit, or addiction—we have to make the marriage happier, so we can stay there, for their sakes, but for our own too. I am not saying this is easy, but it is sure something to be proud of. And the alternatives are worse.

In a Nutshell

- Flush out of your brain the old models:
  - The father as an arrogant king
  - The father as a judge
  - The father as a passive blob
  - The father who is hardly ever there

- Acknowledge that boys need fathers around many hours a day. Do stuff with your son. The path to closeness with sons is activity together. But be sure to talk, too.

- Get involved from pregnancy onward. You can be a presence in his life even in the womb, as a baby, as a little child, and so on.

- Wrestle with your children. Teach your boys, through wrestling, to show care and how to be a good loser or winner. Help them to be excited and also teach them when to calm down.

- Be a firm but safe disciplinarian. Back up your wife and learn firm love techniques. (My book, *More Secrets of Happy Children*, focuses on this.)

- Be involved with daughters, too. Admire them, teach them self-sufficiency. Respect their space and never evaluate their looks, except positively.

- Protect your sons from the violent, the shoddy, and the pseudo-tough—and from having their feelings hurt or hardened over.

- Help to make other men available for your son to learn from and be supported by, especially from fourteen onward.

- Teach your kids that sex is good, but special. Guard them from cheap and exploitive media and situations.

- If you are separated, don't disappear from your kids' lives.

- If your marriage is in trouble, your kids need you to address this. Don't suffer along, but don't walk away from it just because it's sometimes hard. Good marriages are achieved, they don't just happen.

8 Making School Good for Boys

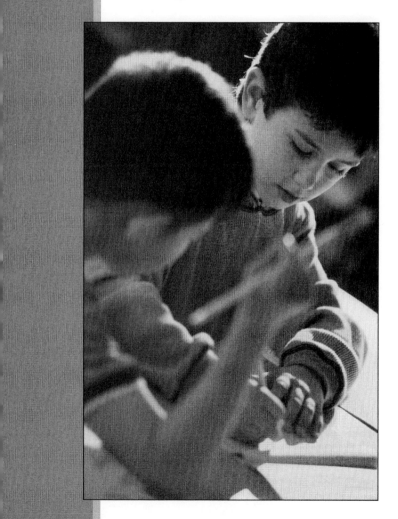

EACH MORNING, IF the weather was fine, the man used to walk his six-year-old son to school. They lived in a quiet country town, and it was a beautiful downhill walk. The boy would skip and run about, pointing out birds, insect life, ripening blackberries. As they drew closer to the school, though, a curious change always came over the boy. A change that saddened the father, for he knew what it was. The boy's voice deepened, his shoulders tensed up, his face got serious. He was putting on the armor all males (in this culture) feel they must wear.

For the last ten years, I have worked with teachers, giving seminars about making school better for boys. I have done this in places as diverse as New Mexico and the British Midlands, Beijing and Capetown, New Zealand and Singapore. Everywhere I hear the same message from teachers: the boys don't live up to their potential. They don't have any aspirations. They get aggressive. They think its "cool to be a fool." The girls are racing ahead, the boys are losing the plot.

Girls racing ahead is not a problem to me—it's a tribute to the efforts educators have made to raise girls' aspirations and unleash their abilities. But boys are doing badly—not just compared to girls, but to themselves; to what we know they could do if they tried, or got the right kind of help.

Several reasons for this have been identified as significant. Boys develop at a different rate than girls. Largely this means they are slower, in language, fine motor skills, and social learning. It's likely they need to start school up to a year later, and move through school being slightly older, in order to keep pace with girls. Men have disappeared from teaching, especially elementary school teaching, so boys don't see learning as a masculine activity. Boys with absent or busy fathers don't aspire to be like Dad. They are governed by the peer group instead. The peer group, unfortunately, is a rather stupid animal that doesn't value learning. The way school is structured seems poorly designed for boys' natures—sitting very still, being quiet, learning passively, doing a lot of fine motor work without a lot of movement or hands-on practical work. And school often lacks the close-up mentoring and one-to-one help that even so-called "primitive" societies were smart enough to provide. Finally, the emotional environment of boy culture in schools is often intimidating and negative. It discourages risk taking or creative behavior.

Professor Ken Rigby, an expert on bullying, has found that one in five boys gets bullied at school at least once per week. A boy who has had a gentle and cooperative start in life at home may find that to be accepted he has to put on macho pretensions, act mean, disparage girls, and even join in acts of bullying.

Rigby describes the pattern in which the boy who is not academically bright (or is not helped to be so) becomes humiliated and angered in the classroom, and recovers his status by bullying others in the schoolyard. Most men remember this from their boyhood—it even happens regularly on *The Simpsons*. Professor Rigby stresses the need for a non-blame approach, which does not make boys angrier still. This by no means implies being soft on bullying. Research on effective school programs has shown that every instance must be confronted, and the playground be made a safe place by teacher presence. The difference is that the problem is solved, and the needs of individual boys resolved so they can move beyond needing to bully.

Rigby believes that the cold and uncaring nature of staff–student interaction contributes to the bullying atmosphere in a school. If the staff bullies the children, they usually bully other children. Principal and teachers set the tone for the school.

The patterns of violence are very predictable in boys' lives. It's known that men who hit their wives or children, or who end up in prison for habitual violence, were easily diagnosable by the fourth grade. A recent study found that a high proportion of boys who behaved aggressively in primary school went on to become drunk drivers. If we can predict these things, then we can stop them happening.

> Men who ended up in prison . . . were easily diagnosable by mid-primary school

SPORT—A DISASTER AREA FOR BODY AND SOUL

Sport often harms those who play it. In a 1994 football match between two prestigious schools in Queensland, Australia, a young man threw a punch at an opposing player. The other boy hit back, striking the side of the first player's head. The boy died from the punch. The teams had been under enormous pressure to win at all costs, "the honor of the school" and a disproportionate amount of attention had been loaded onto what should have been just a game. We know that boys' testosterone levels leap up in these situations and they are prone to more aggressive behavior.

Some coaches today urge boys in contact sports to hit and hurt "as long as they can get away with it." Australian academic Dr. Peter West believes that sport is one of the primary sources of shaping a defective masculine image—arrogant, elitist, violent, unfeeling, individualistic, competitive, and less than fully human. Also, many children now sustain injuries which affect them for life, through overtraining or stress in competing. Many parents now feel ambivalent about sport because of its physical as well as psychological dangers. Yet sport can be so positive in a boy's life, given the right conditions.

SEVEN STEPS TO SCHOOL REFORM

In talking to school staff around the globe, the following seven measures have emerged as the most urgent to take in making school good for boys.

1. Male teachers available at all levels of schooling

Men have disappeared from the teaching profession, especially in elementary schools. Better pay, some positive recruitment, and less paranoia about sexual abuse are needed to reverse this.

Many schools have no men in them at all. At the same time, many boys (perhaps as many as one in three) have no male figures at home and no men active in their lives. School is their last chance to get some surrogate fathering or mentoring. It's very striking to realize that over 80 percent of nonreaders and problem learners are boys. Boys need role models who can show them that learning is a masculine activity. This may be their only chance to experience men who are nonviolent, friendly, good at dealing with misbehavior, and interested in their development. Men can show boys that the world of reading, writing, music, art, and learning is as much a man's as a woman's world.

Some school districts now legislate that all boys (and girls) have access to at least one in three teachers being male during their elementary years. (At the same time, we need more women teachers in senior positions, where they are still underrepresented.)

2. A change in the role of male principals

If the principal is a man—and often he is the only man in the school—it is important that he is accessible for and interactive with the children. He should not be remote, hidden behind administrative roles or continually taken away from school by other demands. Like it or not, he is a father-figure and needs to be a good one.

3. More boyish modes of learning

A lot of school's learning requirements are female oriented. Schools require and reward quiet, cooperative, verbal, fine-motor, indoor, artistic, and passive kinds of activity. We know that boys develop their fine-motor skills more slowly than girls in early primary school—up to a year later in most instances. Boys feel stupid and awkward if expected to produce the same kind of work at the same age. With few exceptions, girls take to education more easily. Boys often have difficulty fitting into a classroom regime and the carrying out of classroom activities.

Education for boys needs to emphasize movement, vigor, and going beyond four walls. They need more exciting or natural activity, which utilizes male qualities instead of repressing them. This should not be limited to sport but extended to science, art, music, reading, and math. Many of these changes would benefit girls too.

4. Releasing women teachers from the need to fight with problem boys

As we've argued earlier, many problems of boys—especially violence and misbehavior—can be attributed to father-hunger. By misbehaving, boys and young men are showing their need to be engaged, valued, and disciplined by strong, loving male figures.

Female teachers often have horrendous, fruitless struggles with "high-need" boys who have little respect for women and who prevent the whole class from learning in the meantime.

Even the most effective and experienced female teachers have told me they feel the boys are needing—virtually asking for—something that they, as women, cannot offer. They can achieve a truce, but still feel that these boys and young men need something more.

Women teachers should not have to struggle continually with boys who need something they cannot provide. Caring but strong mentors should be provided for troubled boys. This should not be just punitive attention but preventive and long-term involvement aimed at giving them a positive, masculine self-image.

5. Training of male teachers in the mentor role

Boys need men—but not just any men. Research by Dr. Peter Downes in England found that four qualities made for the best male teacher—firm, funny, friendly, and focused.

> Four qualities made for the best teacher—funny, firm, friendly, and focused

Boys learned best from a man who was definitely in charge, but not mean or competitive, who was positive, and well organized. They did not like a teacher who was "one of the boys."

Male teachers may be quite poor role models if they have never received the mentoring they now need to impart. Special training is needed. In particular:

- Training in counseling and conflict resolution
- Understanding how boys lacking affection will often develop aggression as a substitute
- The hero-or-villain dynamic in young men—how to redirect energies in constructive ways
- "Tough love" confronting skills—how to teach thinking and problem solving instead of using intimidation as a means of discipline

6. *Use of male-female teaching teams*

Many boys and girls have never seen men and women working together and doing so successfully. Male and female co-principals are usual in Quaker schools, and are very successful.

7. *Gender equity programs—for boys, too*

Many good feminist teachers manage to be committed to the advancement of girls and support and encourage boys as well. Yet this is not always the case. Mothers have told us that they feel their sons as young as kindergarten age are being made to feel inferior, just for being boys. Boys can be a problem, but they do not just willfully choose to be difficult, lacking in social skills, or aggressive. Boys get trapped, just as much as girls do, in low self-esteem and maladaptive behavior. The difference is that their ways of showing this are more of a problem to others. Some feminist teachers would say, "More attention for boys—why should they get any more special attention?" But the fact is, if we want to solve the problems, we have to work from both ends. Most girls will want to know boys, will marry men and work with men. Things won't improve for girls unless boys are helped to make the corresponding changes.

Specific programs for boys, run by male-affirming men and women, are needed to equip boys with the skills to stay alive and be competent socially, at school, at work, as husbands, and as fathers. Boys need to learn fathering and the care of younger children throughout their schooling. Peer support and cross-age tutoring are good examples. Boys themselves appreciate the programs and there are measurable benefits to behavior.

IN CONCLUSION

To our pleasure and relief the reaction from women teachers to all seven of these ideas has been overwhelmingly positive. They have told us, "Yes, this accurately describes what has been missing," "We do have to do something about boys, to complement what is starting to happen with girls," and "Thank goodness we now have some possible answers."

Rather than endlessly playing "more disadvantaged than thou" between the genders, we can recognize that boys and girls need different kinds of help. Schools, at present, by treating all students the same, aren't being fair to either gender. Implementing just a few of these measures would create an improvement in the lot of boys, and before long would be bringing a better kind of young man out into the wider society.

IN A NUTSHELL

School can often be a place of fear and failure for boys. We can make school more boy-friendly in the following ways:

- Making the playground environment safer by stopping bullying and violence by either pupils or teachers.

- Recruiting more of the right kind of men, especially into primary education.

- Stopping over-competitiveness in sport, and reinventing sport for enjoyment, self-development, and exercise—not for the glory of the few.

- Helping teachers develop a co-parenting and mentoring role in boys' emotional development (so that school is an extension of family, and the "whole boy" is the focus and aim).

9 Finding a Job with Heart

MEN LOVE TO work. Late in the evening if you drive through some suburbs, you will always see garage lights on. Inside, groups of men labor over old cars, lovingly modifying, repairing, and maintaining late into the night. Others are busy building furniture in their workshops or working with metal and wood. These are mostly men who have worked hard all day in uninteresting jobs but who, with passion and intelligence, apply themselves at night-time to their real interests. Among the middle classes, the focus shifts to "renovating"— that endless fixing-up of our dwellings that seems to fill the whole of the years from twenty-five to fifty—before we give up and slide downhill again! In other countries (England, for instance), exotic and weird hobbies—from electric trains to orchids, ferret breeding to Shakespearean acting—seem to draw men out from the ordinariness of their daytime lives.

COMRADESHIP

In her remarkable book, *The Continuum Concept*, Jean Liedloff tells of watching a group of Amazon Indian men dragging a heavy dugout canoe up a series of waterfalls. It takes hours. Suddenly, as they grunt their way up the last rapids, one man slips and the heavy canoe slams against the others and is shot by the force of the water hundreds of yards back down the cascade. To her amazement the men roar with laughter, though several are cut and bruised and hours of time have been wasted.

Still chuckling and teasing each other, they climb down the slippery rocks to start over again. Liedloff marvels at the resilience of spirit of Amazon men and women, at the attitude they all seem to share, and wonders how such optimism is trained into their children.

Hard physical work comes naturally to men. Yet it is seen now as something lowly and degrading. D. H. Lawrence described how, in industrial England, the men working in the coal mines took satisfaction and found comradeship in their work and were proud of being good providers. Then schooling was introduced and, rather than working with their fathers, the boys began going to school. There they were taught by white-collared teachers that their fathers' world—the sweaty, difficult world of physical labor—was demeaning and that they should through education rise to a, "higher" world. We don't want to earn our living through sweat, but at the same time, something is lost when we never share the companionship and pride of hard physical work.

Fit to be tied

I borrowed a tie from a friend down the road . . . and won the fellowship

Here's a personal story. In 1979 I applied for a Churchill Fellowship, in the faint hope of being able to study in the U.S. I was granted an interview. At the time I was twenty-six, idealistic, still very much a hippy, rebellious and socially awkward. Minutes before the interview, I suddenly thought about what to wear. I called into a neighbors' house, borrowed a suit and tie, went to the interview, and won the fellowship! I was lucky—it was a small town, and several of the interview panel knew my work—but without the tie, I don't think I would have "qualified."

A tie symbolizes something very profound—a willingness to fit in or to submit. Every day outside any courthouse you

THE DEMON

WHEN I AWOKE THIS MORNING
EXHAUSTED FROM MY REST
A DEMON DARK AND TERRIBLE
WAS SITTING ON MY CHEST.

HE PINNED ME TO THE MATTRESS
AND SEIZED ME BY THE HEAD
HE PRESSED HIS KNEES AGAINST MY HEART
AND OVERTURNED THE BED.

HE DRAGGED ME TO THE MIRROR
AND SHOWED ME MY DISGRACE
THEN TOOK A RAZOR IN HIS CLAW
AND DRAGGED IT DOWN MY FACE

SOME FADED RAGS HE BOUND AROUND
MY SHOULDERS AND MY HIPS
AND POURED A CUP OF STEAMING MUCK
BETWEEN MY FADED LIPS

AND THEN HE TOOK THOSE WILTED LIPS
AND IN HIS EVIL STYLE
HE PARALYSED THE CORNERS UP
INTO A PLEASANT SMILE

A MASTERPIECE IN WICKEDNESS
THIS LAST SADISTIC JOKE
HE SENDS ME OUT INTO THE WORLD
A SMILING SORT OF BLOKE.

will see people standing in suits and ties who look like they have never dressed that way before in their lives. No one is fooled by this. Everyone—the suit-wearers, the judges—knows that this is a ruse—to "look" like you are trying to be a respectable person. But the gesture is important. It says, "See, I am willing to go through the motions. I will be a good boy."

At work a tie says, "I am willing to put up with this discomfort" and therefore "I am willing to put up with other indignities and constraints to get and keep this job." (Can I polish your boots with my tie?) It's important to see a tie for what it is. It's a slave collar.

Class is a funny thing. Many men have long discovered, too late, that rising in the class hierarchy does not make you freer. If you are a blue-collar worker, the company wants your body but your soul is usually your own. A white-collar worker is supposed to hand over his spirit as well. There's a scene in the Australian film *The Fringe Dwellers*, where the Aboriginal men sit together making jokes about the poor white man spending his weekends mowing the lawn and washing the car.

It's not just the tie—a whole uniform goes with it (interesting word, uniform). The popular term for the men who attend to the boring details of the business world is "suits." Richard Gere, as the millionaire in *Pretty Woman*, strikes a deal and leaves the details to "the suits" to tidy up. Suits (and the men who wear them) are all about a lack of individuality.

Ride the commuter planes and trains between capital cities any morning at seven A.M. or late in the evening and you will be amazed at herds of look-alike, grey-faced men, moving endlessly to and fro across the country in the dreadful lifestyle of the "executive." They might be flying business class, they are first off the plane, into the Club lounges, but no one could envy them. They are privileged eunuchs, leading a dry and joyless life.

BEWARE THE MORTGAGE TRAP

How does this all happen? How do intelligent men become enslaved? After all, no one forces us to compete in the rat race. Our system has one outstanding way of holding men in place—it's called a mortgage. A mortgage is a good idea gone wrong. It isn't the invention of bankers—the idea of owing for a lifetime has a long tradition. The feasters at a New Guinean wedding, for example, consume so many pigs and yams that a young man will spend his life repaying the debt. Amish people in America will gather in their hundreds to build a large, beautiful barn in a single day, which will set up a newlywed couple for a lifetime of farming. The young couple will in turn help out at many other barn-raisings in the course of their lifetime. This is a system of mutual support, with a mutual obligation, which has kept the Amish safe, prosperous, recession-proof, and with low divorce rates for several centuries.

The mortgage system allows you to have a house or apartment from the start of your adult life and to spend your life paying for it. Your obligation is not to people but to institutions. (Lose your job, fail to pay, and faceless institutions will throw you out.) When you go for that vital interview at the bank (wearing your tie, of course!) you walk out with a hundred thousand dollars. It's a miracle! But something else happens, something they don't tell you about. You leave a testicle behind! The bank manager keeps it in a jar in his safe, along with all the others! If ever in your life you get the urge to do something risky, exciting, different, or adventurous, chances are you will not because you won't have the balls to do it!

Somehow, to be a free man, you have to escape this trap. You could live in the country where houses cost less. You could stop competing with your neighbors and drive the oldest car in your street. You could give your children more of your time, instead of a private school education. You could take a year off and just think it all over!

PUTTING THE HEART BACK INTO WORK

It isn't the fact of working that kills you. It's the nature of the work that is the problem. If you do a job that lacks heart, it will kill you. The strongest predictor of life expectancy in a man— greater than diet, lifestyle, or income—is *whether he likes his job.* Two factors—the lack of real purpose and the lack of personal control—are the main problems.

Our ancestors laughed as they worked and sang; they enjoyed the rush of the hunt, the steady teamwork of digging for vegetables, or the discovery of a honey-filled tree. Watch any documentary or archival footage of preliterate people and you will see this clearly. Life was often hard but it was rarely without laughter. In time, though, cultures evolved away from the forest and the coast and into the village and the town. We did the work that others decided, and it became a grind—increasingly repetitive. It was a numbing of human senses and a subjugation of ourselves beneath the need just to survive. Today, work has become more comfortable but not more fulfilling. It's still a separate compartment in life—something you tolerate in exchange for "real" living in the time left over from doing your job, getting to your job, and recovering from your job! Work today drives an unhealthy wedge into the very core of our life. The time has come to heal it.

Most people today do work they do not much like—jobs that are beneath them. When I was a kid in school, we had "career guidance." Its ostensible aim was to help you find something you liked to do. But underneath it all we dimly sensed the real purpose. Since you had to work to purchase the good life, the aim was just to find the best paying job you could *tolerate.*

We easily pass this on to our kids. "Get good grades, your future depends on it." Yet the purpose of adolescence is to find what you really love to do. Once you find it, you must learn to do it well enough, so that it will feed you. You will either be happy, or rich and happy! The aim is to have work that makes you jump out of bed in the morning, keen to get started. This is not as hard as you might have been led to believe.

THE EIGHT LEVELS OF FULFILLING WORK

What follows are eight criteria for assessing your working life. If you achieve any one of these, you deserve to feel good. If you feel bored and stuck in your work, then look to the next stage as your guide. These are not for use in comparing self and others. They are measures of individual heroism. A brain-injured man learning to clean his own backside can show more courage than a national hero.

1. Do you do your share?

This begins early. Even a three-year-old can and should contribute around the house. You can be an unemployed teenager, living at home, and still add to the well-being of your household. Perhaps you care for younger children, cook meals, fix up the house, grow food in a garden, take classes, travel and learn about the world, as money allows. You can feel proud that you contribute as well as receive. Remember, it was business tycoons who caused America's recession. What we need are more people who can simply carry their own weight.

2. Can you support yourself?

If you have a job or earn an income of some kind then you are not drawing on the resources of the nation. They can be used to care for others who haven't that accomplishment. You are a plus to society. This is the second step on the way. If this is all you ever do, you are an asset.

3. Is your job one that allows you to improve the lives of others?

Many unglamorous jobs—bus drivers, shopkeepers, or doctors' receptionists, for example—have an important daily impact on hundreds of people they deal with. By realizing that your real work is the contact you make with people, and by doing so in a friendly, interested way (not just carrying out the mechanics of your task), you can have a positive effect on the people you deal with and the people they deal with in turn.

> It isn't enough to be successful, you have to ask yourself—successful at what?

4. Are you a provider for others?

Even if you only have a job that is very routine, supporting others is an achievement. Partner, children, and family can benefit and get a good start under the umbrella created by your being the provider. You are a life-giver.

5. Does your work provide an infrastructure for the work of others?

Does your job create other jobs, give leadership and structure, opportunity and growth to other people? Your work or business may provide a niche for others that otherwise might not have existed.

6. Do you train and develop other people, enhancing their lives and futures?

No one is grown-up when they begin work. We all need mentors and father-figures in the workplace, not just bosses. We need men and women who have our interests at heart. Sit down and write out the qualities of the kind of boss you would like to work for. Then see if you can match up to these qualities. Being a mentor to others can be the most satisfying aspect of any job.

7. Does your work help protect the earth, its people, and its life?

Doctors have an ancient rule—at least, do no harm. If we all applied this in our jobs, it would be interesting. For instance, you may make a good living distributing a farm chemical that is banned in Europe yet protected in the U.S. by powerful lobbying. Doing this would not be illegal, but clearly (like the plumbers at Auschwitz, say) you are part of something fundamentally bad. Would a caring shopkeeper refuse to sell cigarettes—to anyone? A movie maker needs to ask, what kind of movies does the world need? The ad man, what kind of ads? A journalist, what kind of news items? A real man has to look at these questions. It isn't enough just to be successful. You have to ask, successful at what?

8. Does your work use your innate abilities and talents so that it is unique and powerful in its effect on the world?

Some men know how to teach children, others can heal pain, carve sculptures, make violins, ride a wave, kick a ball, lay cement, design glorious buildings, make new laws. When your job is also your creativity brought to life, then you do wonderful work.

Every man has creative activity coiled up inside him. How can you tell? You will know—an unexpressed urge will actually hurt you if it isn't let out. Begin in a small way, and see where it leads.

SAME JOB, DIFFERENT ATTITUDE

Realistically, for many men, the trick is finding the heart in the work you already do. Think about your job. How would you go about removing the façade that is traditionally built up in your line of work, so that you can be more of the real you? I recently saw a real estate agent manage the sale of a house for an old lady whose husband lay dying in the hospital. She was so caring, for seller and buyers that everyone became friends and went to the funeral together. I have a friend who is Australia's top orthodontist. He tells a quarter of the people who walk through his door that they don't need his services. They would be wasting their money. I once watched a shop assistant, a young man of about twenty or so, so gentle and tender in his handling of a confused old lady that it brought tears to my eyes. These people are different from the norm, and they transform the banal situation into magic. They have the grace that comes from some inner sense of what matters.

I don't think all work can be converted in this way. Some basically negative jobs, like politics as it is currently practiced, environmentally damaging work, or dishonest work like some kinds of selling, breed a paranoia that twists in on itself, however much the man denies that he gives a damn. Like St. Paul on the road to Damascus, there comes a time to say, I quit.

Capitalism has outlasted communism, but that doesn't mean it actually works. In fact—as several very well-qualified commentators, from Schumacher to J.K. Galbraith, have pointed out—it depends on constant, cancer-like growth, which will make the world unliveable. If mainstream men keep doing what they are doing—earning and spending more and more—then the world will simply choke to death. When mainstream men can learn to live with less, and derive their pleasure from doing and being instead of from owning, then it might be possible to have a post-capitalist economy that actually works—and is lots more fun to live in.

RETIREMENT—AN INSULT AND A WASTE

Years ago I heard David Mowaljarlai, a Kimberley Aboriginal elder, speaking about the life-cycle of a man in traditional society. One of the older (white) men present asked whether an Aboriginal elder ever retired. David smiled and described the ceremony his people would conduct each year, in which the leader of a clan would have to climb to the top of a pole placed in the ground, thus proving that he was still strong enough to lead. I thought at the time how subtle a device this was, since most people would assume that the old man would want to stay as leader. And yet an old man would actually have a choice whether he made it to the top of the pole or not. "Damn, I guess I just can't make it this year!"

Retirement is a source of some pain and ambivalence among many men. Perhaps this was the questioner's thought too, as he asked, "What then?"

Mowaljarlai searched in his mind for the right word. "I don't know what you call it in English. The old fella—he becomes no longer the leader, he's the 'manual.'"

For a moment I thought he meant manual labor. I envisaged a disgraced elder cleaning up around the camp.

People looked blank. Mowaljarlai tried to explain. "You know, like the book you get with your car." Someone caught on. "Oh, the manual—the instruction book." "Yes," said Mowaljarlai, "when the new leader, he comes across something he can't handle, he hasn't seen before, he goes and consults the 'manual!'"

In American factories and car plants, many older managers and foremen were fired in the 1980s as accountants and economic rationalism ran things by the "bottom line." But things started to go wrong. Soon, according to *In Search of Excellence* author Tom Peters, these old men were brought back, on high pay and short hours, to walk around the plant and look things over. They had the sixth sense, the subtle knowledge, to tell when a machine was about to go out of phase, or an interpersonal problem was developing to crisis point. They could act before the problem was a problem because they knew how to read the signs. There is no substitute, you see, for experience.

IN A NUTSHELL

- Burn your tie or use it to tie up the tomato plants.

- Either find a job you can believe in or find something to believe in about your job.

- If you're a boss, realize that you are a father-figure. You are there to nourish and care for your people, so they can do their jobs. Give more positive feedback. Vary your expectations to suit individuals. Share your vision. Ask people their opinions.

- Confront irresponsibility. Don't put people down. Discipline in private, praise in public.

- If you're in a team, realize that by dropping competition, you can achieve amazing goals, especially if they are goals you can believe in.

- Love, fun, and idealism have as much place at work as in any other aspect of life.

- If you must retire, don't retire from life. Become an elder. Above all, stay involved.

OTHER VOICES

Don't Burn Your Tie

Walker Feinlein, Professor of Textile Anthropology at the University of Hobart, strongly counsels against burning your tie in a fit of masculinist fervor. Bra-burning in the Sixties was largely a media creation, he explained, arising out of an accident with a faulty cigarette lighter. Alternative uses for ties include using them to stake the tomato plants, throwing a couple in the car trunk for use as an emergency fanbelt, or tying several ties together to create a colorful drum strap for those all-night sessions!

Michael Leunig, Australia's best-known cartoonist (in an interview with Caroline Jones)

Yes, I think . . . men have become enslaved. Possibly it's the industrialization process. They've become removed from Nature, which kept them connected to feelings. Zorba the Greek is not easily found amongst contemporary men. (Laughs) They seem to be enslaved and somewhat castrated, I think, and the fact that men have to get up in the morning and go off to work (this is how it was traditionally). . . . I used to see my father do this: get up at 5.30 A.M., go off to a cold meatworks, come home late, exhausted, every day of his life. He just wasn't in the race; he didn't have a chance in many ways. He had to be tough; he wasn't allowed to have those feelings.

And I think this has suited women to some extent too, or a lot of women I mean, just as feminism seemed to women to be throwing off the role that was allotted to them, I think this has yet to happen to men. Men are carrying so much expectation and misunderstanding. It hasn't been easy to be a male through the feminist years because to be constantly told that all men are rapists and all men are exploitative, and all men are pigs, and blah blah blah, . . . while one recognizes the truth in part of that, it's not good, it doesn't help men at all, it's made men retreat. Men have lost their nerve a bit, as they need to, but I just hope it goes on and they rise up a bit against— not women, because they need to love women and to care for women, women aren't the enemy. Maybe it's a sort of capitalism, maybe it's consumerism; maybe it's all these things, that "the system" as they say, has enslaved men. They've been made into a "work unit," an economic unit, they have to keep earning all this money. (Caroline adds: And keep this system going which, as you pointed out earlier, really isn't serving us terribly well, it would seem now, and that's heartbreaking. . . .)

It's a terrible thing. . . . If it was serving us well, if we had marvelous schools and it was all a bit more humanistic, and fulfilling, then, well, let's work hard. But all this hard work, and distress, and this debt—for what? So you can watch some cheap video, and eat junk food, and look at your neighborhood falling apart, and the shopping center full of plastic signs and noise and carelessness? Men need to, . . . I think men often define themselves in some way or feel connected to this world by their skills, their dexterity, the way they can make things and do things. They're becoming more useless, it seems, more enslaved, more trapped. They sit at desks, and they've got to look good—they've got to look so damn good now, and so neat and pressed, and the hair's got to be just right, and they've got to smell nice and stare at a screen all day. The regimentation is appalling, and what does this do to the human spirit? What is it doing to the spirit of man? If there be an essential male psyche or something, I imagine it's having a terrible effect.

When do you get the fullest sense of being who you are?

I like being in the dirt a bit, getting my hands dirty, or something like that. What about sex? I mean, why does no one mention sex when they're asked what they most like to do? That's an important thing I do. I like sex, I like eating, I like going to bed at night—those fundamental things. These are terribly central and important. I like gardening, I like digging a hole. I like to construct something, I like to paint . . . I think those things are sacred, and they are common to us all, I would think. Oh, and this other thing . . . I think that people are deprived somewhat by modern life; the chance to be of some clear value to the society or to a person, to save someone's life, or to pick someone off the road or to help them. You watch people in a country town if there's a bushfire. Everyone just leaps to get out and do a bit for each other, and it brings out this lovely vitality, and people discover all levels within themselves.

I am not a mechanism, an assembly of various sections.
And it is not because the mechanism is working wrongly,
*   that I am ill.*
I am ill because of wounds to the soul, to the deep
*   emotional self*
and the wounds to the soul take a long, long time, only
*   time can help*
and patience, and a certain difficult repentance
long, difficult repentance, realization of life's mistake,
*   and the freeing oneself*
from the endless repetition of the mistake
which mankind at large has chosen to sanctify.
—D. H. Lawrence, Healing

I have chosen to emphasize what I think is believed to be the most central source of men's alienation—the absence of a sense of abiding meaning or, as I prefer to say, vocation, in our lives.

—Sam Keen in *Fire in the Belly*

. . . forty-eight percent of American men are now employed by one of the top ten giant corporations, or by the US government.

Without work, all life goes rotten. But when work is soulless, life stifles and dies.

—Albert Camus

10 **Real Male Friends**

TWO FARMERS STAND in the dusty yard of a property. One is a neighbor, come to say goodbye, the other is watching as the last of his furniture is packed onto a truck. The farm looks bare—livestock gone, machinery sold. Two teenagers stand by the car, the wife sits inside it, eyes averted.

The two men have farmed alongside each other for thirty years, fought wildfires, driven through the night with injured children, eaten thousands of meals, drunk gallons of coffee, and cared for each other's wives and kids as their own. They have shared good times and bad. Now, one is leaving, bankrupt. He will go to live in the city, where his wife will support them by cleaning motels.

"Well," says the man. "I'll be off then."

"Yeah," says the other. "Thanks for coming over."

"Look us up sometime."

"Yeah, I reckon."

And they climb into their vehicles and leave. And while their wives will correspond for years to come, these men will never exchange words again.

So much unspoken. So much that would help the healing to take place from this terrible turn of events. What pain would flow out if one were to say, "Listen, you've been the best friend a guy could want," and looked the other straight in the eye as he said it. Or if they had spent a long evening together with their wives, full of "remember whens" punctuated by

167

tears and easing laughter. If, instead of standing stiff-armed and choked, they could have had a long, strong hug from which to draw strength and assurance, as they faced the hardship their futures would bring. The farmer leaving the land will not find the opportunity for any of these supports, comforts, or appreciations. He will be a massive risk for suicide, alcoholism, cancer, or accident, as he twists up inside to suppress the emotions his body feels.

Men, you see, don't have friends—at least not in those countries cursed with an Anglo-Saxon heritage. Instead we have "buddies," with whom we share a secret agreement on which subjects we never discuss! A subtle and elaborate code governs the humor, the put-downs, the ways in which serious feeling or vulnerability is deflected. All this is well known and often written about. So it's time to make a change.

Little boys start out warm and affectionate. You will see them in the younger grades at school, arms about each other. And at this age they still are tender and kind to younger children, comfortable about being with girls, and able to cry over a dead pet or a sad story. So what goes wrong? Let's find out.

PROVING YOU'RE A MAN

We've already said that men are absent from the lives of little boys. So are older boys, since in our society we isolate each age group and expect them to mix only with same-age, same-sex children. This is an odd arrangement, since little boys love to be around older boys in every village and slum and tribe around the world. By comparison, the world of the little boy in elementary school is a harsh and scary one. Because the older children have not been taught to nurture the younger ones, but rather to see them as competition for limited adult affection, the playground is violent and mean. It becomes the law of the jungle—the kind of conditions portrayed in the book *Lord of the Flies*.

Paul Whyte, of the Sydney Men's Network in Australia, uses an exercise to help women understand what it is like to be a boy in the schoolyard culture. He asks them to imagine that their membership of their gender depends on their being able to physically defend themselves against others of their gender. Imagine, for a minute, if being a woman meant having to fight, physically, with any woman who came along and having to hold your ground against her. If you couldn't do this, you would be beaten and you would be accused of not being a woman! This is life for many boys at school. Verbal attacks, if not actual violence is an ever present threat, and proving yourself adequate, through physical strength, is a continual issue. This portrayal certainly describes my childhood. How about yours?

> Imagine if being a woman meant having to fight . . . with any woman who came along

PROVING YOU'RE NOT GAY

Because their masculinity is not taught or proactively developed by the men of the community, boys feel a strong need to prove their masculinity. Most parents will notice how their son drops his voice to a deeper pitch when his friends are around—or refuses to kiss his baby sister goodnight if a friend is visiting.

Into this already volatile situation, especially as puberty arrives, comes a strange twist. The existence of homosexuality as a biological fact in the human race, combined with many people's inability to be comfortable with this variation in type, means that the dread of being thought to be gay hangs over the head of any boy who is different in any way from the norm. The risk is great, and varies from being rejected, ridiculed, beaten, or even killed, depending on the severity of the culture. Our non-acceptance of gays is tough on a youngster experiencing homosexual leanings, but it also exacts a severe price on every straight young man. It leads to the self-censoring of any kind of warmth, creativity, affection, or emotionality among the whole male gender. A boy thinks "If I'm not 'macho,' then I might be seen to be gay." Children may exhibit this fear even when they are not even aware of what being gay means. They just know its something not to be.

When we oppress gay people, we oppress ourselves as well. No one feels free to be themselves.

THE SCOURGE OF COMPETITION

Competitiveness, as a personality trait, stems from compulsively searching for approval that never comes. Even winning, as many top athletes find, is not enough. Yet given adequate approval from their mentors, boys and men do not have this compulsion to impress—they settle down to learning for its own sake, less concerned with being biggest and best. There are parts of the world where competition simply does not exist—Native American children often help each other to take tests, for example, and Balinese people are gloriously creative and artistic without any sense of being better than others.

Everyone agreed that condoms were a great idea except for one thing—while men came in different sizes, condoms only came in one standard size. Manufacturers had figured out early that no self-respecting man would walk into a chemist shop and ask for a six pack of small condoms!

The conversation turned quiet at this point as each person made their own inner reflections. Finally someone hit on an answer. The smallest size could be called "large!" What about the larger sizes? The atmosphere became ribald at this stage. It was finally agreed after many alternatives that there should be three sizes of condom—"large," "huge" and "Oh my God!"

(Adapted from a story in the *Whole Earth Review*)

Competition is a continual undercurrent of men's lives. One man wrote to me

"I notice when I sit down in a public place, beside a swimming pool, or at a park, I relax and feel good if there is no one else around. If another man arrives, I first run a check that he is no physical threat—that he is not about to mug me. No one has ever mugged me or hurt me since childhood, but the feeling still lives. (Women understand this reflex, for different reasons.) Then I get to assessing whether he is stronger, has better clothes, or is more athletic. If he is with a woman, I look for signs that she doesn't really like him! If the parking lot is within view, I check out his car for comparison with my own. Even if he is friendly and a conversation starts, I have to fight the urge to mention my achievements, what an important person I am— to subtly start winning the contest. The inner competition never stops—I seem caught in a basically hostile and insecure obsession with comparisons.

I am now retraining myself to change this damaging and isolating pattern. I am teaching myself to see other men as brothers, with good things to give and to receive. I have always felt this warmth and friendliness toward women, but why not men too? This is leading to a huge change in attitude and a huge boost in my enjoyment of half the human race."

Males who are denied appropriate physical affection with other males while growing up become people who never mature. In fact many men who are so denied will strongly repress their need for manly affection. You can see these men in any football game or boxing match. They seem to thrive on the violent aspects of male contact, while distancing themselves from any form of intimacy.

When men are allowed to freely experience the love and support of other men, they begin to question competition in our society. This questioning engenders a willingness to engage in more service-oriented projects and activities whose aim is to nurture and protect others. Here lies the potential for a whole different kind of man.

BEYOND COMPETITION

The Xervante people of Brazil divide manhood into eight stages of growth. These peer groups stay very close throughout life, and they are also assisted and tutored by those in the group higher up in the sequence. Each year the Xervante hold running races for each age group in turn. These races look like a contest but they are not. When a runner falters or trips, the others pick him up and run with him. The group always finishes in a pack.

In fact it's not a race at all in the sense we mean it, though everyone puts in a huge effort. It's a celebration of manhood—an expression of surplus vitality. This is a culture that has survived thousands of years by cooperation. They don't have to prove they are men, they celebrate that they are men. Marvin Allen says it beautifully: "I defy anyone, anywhere in the world, to 'prove' that they're a man." In fact it's a ridiculous concept. Women wouldn't entertain the concept of "proving" they are women.

Friends make life infinitely more worth living. They help to structure your time. They show you that you belong and can be cared about. Perhaps this is why men traditionally cook at barbecues. It's a declaration that "men can feed you too." If you don't believe this, listen to the banter that takes place between men and women over the quality of the burgers and hot dogs!

A man who lacks a network of friends is seriously impaired in living his life. Friends alleviate the neurotic overdependence on a wife or girlfriend for every emotional need. If a man, going through a rough time gets help from his friends as well as his partner, then the burden is shared. If his problems are with his partner (as they often are) then his friends can help him through, talk sense into him, stop him from acting stupidly, and help him to release his grief.

A MALE-OUT—MEN SUPPORTING MEN IN CRISIS

Some years ago, in a large government department in the city where I live, a man in his forties was given a notice of dismissal. He had been a dedicated, professional worker and his boss did not have the guts to tell him personally. Instead, this man and several colleagues received a photocopied dismissal letter, and that was that.

> They rostered themselves so someone was always awake with the man

The man became increasingly irrational and in his lunch break went out and purchased a gun. He shredded work documents, and went home in an emotional state, greatly alarming his wife and young children.

Several friends conferred about what to do. They went to his house, taking food and sleeping bags, and spent the next couple of days living there, while his wife and children were sent elsewhere. They rostered themselves so that someone was always awake and with the man—who was too agitated to sleep very much. By the Sunday afternoon, after much talking, crying, and holding, the man thanked his friends for stopping him from "making an idiot" of himself and began to make concrete plans for his future. The friends stayed in touch and checked that things were in fact going well. His family came back home a few days later, and his life has progressed well.

The friends knew somehow that this was their job—it was a man's issue. Male friends can do these things where wives and other women probably cannot. Other men know how you are feeling. Men have issues—about being a hero/provider for instance—which do not have a female equivalent. Sometimes only other men can help you learn about the ongoing process of being a man.

COMMUNICATING FEELINGS

Millions of women complain about their husband's lack of feeling, his woodenness. Men themselves often feel numb and confused about what they really want. Pop psychology books like the Mars and Venus genre tell us to just accept this. But what if men's inarticulateness simply comes from a lack of sharing opportunities with other men? If men talked to each other more, perhaps they'd understand themselves better. Perhaps with this practice, they could better articulate to their wives what is going on for them. It seems entirely possible that only in the company of other men can men begin to activate their hearts. Michael Meade says that just as men's voices have a different tone, so do their feelings. We have more than enough feelings, but they are not the same as women's feelings. Once activated, we have no trouble expressing ourselves.

THE DEHUMANIZING OF MEN

How many of you here are tall, rich, you know, successful, powerful, got an eight-inch dong, got hair on your chest, slender, muscular, always in control . . . has anybody . . . we've got one over here! Only man here!!

There's a new definition of a man here, and it has at least—at least—as much emphasis on loving and nurturing, as on providing and protecting.

—Marvin Allen

Men get set up in a serious double bind by the larger society. They are asked—especially of late—to be more intimate and more sensitive. However, they are still coached in the possibility of being sent to war, still expected to be tough when needed. We don't actually want men who are weaker—just men who can shift between tough, and tender, as the situation requires, which is a considerable skill.

A woman at a conference summed this up very well . . .

> I have been married twice, and had several other relationships that ended badly. Like most women I have always 'listened' to men, but until today I never heard them. I have never heard men talk to other men with such depth and love. And I never imagined what it was like for men to live with the knowledge that they must be prepared to kill, or with the actual horror of battle. This weekend I feel like I have been in a room with giants. I thank you for letting me listen.

One writer described traveling with four friends in a car and coming across a serious accident scene. The men piled out of the car, stopped traffic, pulled injured people out of vehicles, staunched serious bleeding, and did their best to comfort the family of two people who had been killed outright. It was a remote place, and three hours had passed before it was all over.

"What I would like to have seen," the writer said later, "was a newspaper headline reading 'Five men control their feelings in order to save lives in highway carnage.'" He was pointing out that controlling one's feelings is a very valuable part of male make-up. It has great survival value, and all women, deep down, count on it. Being able to also let go of those feelings, when the time is right, is another matter entirely.

AT A GATHERING OF MEN

A group of men sits in an afternoon gathering, part of a larger conference on the family. Women have been asked not to attend this meeting. The atmosphere in the room is different from the other seminars of the day—slightly somber, a little charged. A middle-aged woman who is lost puts her head in the door, immediately senses the atmosphere, mumbles an apology, and disappears.

It's my job to lead this seminar. I sit quietly, getting comfortable with the room, settling down into my body. I have started thousands of seminars and talks, and know not to disperse my own energy trying too hard to be "friendly."

When the time comes, I begin to speak and the group slowly warms up. Unlike the vitality and the slight sense of indignation you will find in a gathering of women, in a men's group there is great reserve, even fear. This is lightened a little by banter and warmth from some of the older, more experienced men. As a man in my forties, I stand midway—no longer as brash or superficially confident as I once was, and also aware of the depth of experience that lies in the room. So I speak first to the older men and thank them for coming. I acknowledge explicitly that they have lived longer and deeper than I have. I ask for their help to make the session a success. I also welcome younger men, and thank them for their freshness and energy. I hope they can do a better job when their time comes.

The discussion follows a kind of natural gravitational pull which, at this time in men's history, seems to be the way forward. We talk first about what is not working—rifts with fathers, painful experiences in marriage, parenthood, health. The invitation is for men to tell parts of their experience and simply listen to each other. One after another, men speak. As they speak, quietly and simply, eyes fill and men begin to cry. From time to time we break into smaller clusters of men, then return to share conclusions. It is hard to stop people talking. At the end, no one wants to leave. It is another hour after the appointed time before the last man shares a long hug with me and goes on his way.

There is a pressure inside men which has been building up for a very long time. It's nothing complicated—just, "How is your life going?" Yet this kind of conversation does not happen at a bar or the gym, or the Rotary club or church meeting. So the opportunity for a very natural and necessary part of men's soul development is missing from our lives. Imagine how tense women would become if they could never talk to other women. Understanding this, perhaps men's tension and numbness makes more sense. We've held back from each other for so long.

GRIEF

Grief expert Mal McKissock has said that when men shut down their feelings, it starts to kill them. A bereaved man is eight times more likely to die in the two-year period following bereavement than a man with family intact. If a child in a family dies—a crib death, for instance—there is a 70 percent likelihood that the parents' marriage will not survive the loss. We simply—and urgently—must provide a means for men to express their grief. McKissock explains that failing to grieve leads to a loss of passion in the whole of life. No one wants to stay married to a block of wood, and so marriage disintegrates. Wives and partners have their own pain, and so often cannot provide what is needed. Mal McKissock believes that failing to feel one single emotion (in this case, sadness) leads to a shutdown in the full spectrum of feelings—anger, fear, and warmth and love. This passion is what most men have lost, and this is also what we stand to gain.

Crying is a simple physical act. When we cry our body produces its own healing endorphins that wash through our brain, healing the losses we've sustained. Once we've wept we can breathe freely, see clearly, feel the love of others, and face the world again.

The better a man takes care of himself during these dark

times, the sooner he passes through the dark night. The more damage and denial he does to himself, the longer he will take to heal, and the deeper will be the mistakes he makes along the way. More hearts will be broken in his attempts to heal his broken heart.

A man once came to see me, who had lost his father through illness at the age of eight. His mother committed suicide two years later, and the children found her body when they came home from school. He and his younger brothers were split up and sent to various relatives and rarely saw each other. By the time I met him, he was a highly successful businessman, but was troubled by sudden rages which had lost him a number of employees. He had two failed marriages and was just holding on in a third. By now he knew that the problem was in him, and was ready to talk. All he really needed to do was tell the story and express the grief that went with it. A simple, profound act that he had never done, with anyone, since childhood. As he told his story, softly and slowly, he would suddenly be overcome with great washes of tears and sobbing. Then he would quietly go on. Gradually the most extraordinary feeling of peace came into the room where we were sitting. It's an experience I will never forget.

FUN AND FRIENDSHIP

The other reason for male friends is to have fun. The kind of fun that is noisy, energetic, affectionate, ribald, accepting, and free.

> We called ourselves SPERM (the Society for the Protection and Encouragement of Righteous Manhood).
> —Sam Keen, *Fire in the Belly*

Some teenage boys near where I live did an unusual thing— they had enjoyed some camping trips on the banks of the

Huon River, and decided they wanted to build a wooden boat and sail down the river. Since they were young men, rather than children, their parents gave the project their blessing. With the help of one of the fathers, they found a shed to work in, scrounged materials, worked weekends, saved money, and the boat gradually took shape.

Things did not always go smoothly between them. One young man often failed to match the monetary contribution of the others, and added to the insult by borrowing money from them for other purposes. Since several of them had taken part-time jobs to raise funds, they were angry after a time and decided to confront him:

"You aren't pulling your weight. You're using us!"

Because of the bond that already existed between them, and the firm but unaggressive way they tackled him, he did not storm off. He thought it over, got a job, and paid back what he owed. He gained in the character department.

Another of the young boat builders had trouble with overbearing parents with high expectations. The others noted his growing depression and consulted their parents about how to help. They decided to simply tell their friend up front: "Listen, man, you only have to live with your parents for another year. Hang in there and finish school. Then your life's your own. You do what you want to do with your life. You can always live here in the boathouse!"

These were islands of seriousness in a sea of good times. Everyone's lives are eased, stabilized, and supported by these friendships. Why shouldn't all men—young and old—have such a safety net in their lives? It could help them avoid all kinds of disasters.

IN A NUTSHELL

- Not having many good men around, boys doubt their manhood.

- They tend to fight and compete with other boys.

- Competing just makes us lonelier.

- Men are the best people to help a man in crisis.

- Men in men's groups discover they have so much in common that was hidden away, and experience an exhilarating sense of relief.

- Many new possibilities for living more courageously, being calmer and steadier as a father and partner, and reshaping the culture, arise from men supporting each other in this way.

11 The Wild Spirit of Man

IN THIS CHAPTER, we will look at three of the deeper concepts of men's spiritual development. These are—Initiation, the Wild Man, and the Time of Ashes.

> For this is the journey that men make. To find themselves. If they fail in this, it doesn't matter what else they find.
> —James A. Michener, *The Fires of Spring*

RELIGION, SPIRIT, AND MAN

Throughout history, all the peoples of the earth have practiced some kind of religion. In fact, it has always been a central force in their lives. The caves of Lascaux with their beautiful animal paintings are our earliest records of masculine ritual. In many societies in pre-history, (including the aboriginal culture of Australia where I live), religious practices took up more than 70 percent of the time and energy of the older men and women. We have to either conclude that these people were primitive, superstitious, and therefore stupid, or we have to acknowledge that there was a purpose and life-supporting function in these activities, even though we may only dimly understand what that could be.

Our logical minds are limited; they were designed for simple tasks, not for understanding the universe. Yet at the same time, we can sense a unity and wholeness to creation which, when we are in tune with it, makes our lives flowing, unselfish, and gives us courage and purpose. Feeling connected to all that is around us, not separate, selfish, or isolated, is the heart of spirituality.

Religion is our attempt to strengthen and maximize people's ability to be spiritual. In spite of the divisions and bigotries that religion can foster, the forces of good—from working with prisoners on death row, to campaigning for world peace—have a strong religious component. And the most potent and effective men and women—from Nelson Mandela to the Dalai Lama to Aung San Suu Kyi—are those with religious underpinnings to their life.

Today we have very little ritual in our lives—we think it has no use. Yet even when we use the term "empty ritual" we are acknowledging that ritual can also be "full." Group events, such as ceremonies and gatherings, are important ways to help each other stay focused on what matters, put a spiritual depth into our lives, and pull our perspective back to the big picture and away from trivial concerns. If people decided not to bother holding funerals, it would be a devastating thing for the mental health of relatives and friends. It would say nothing mattered about this person's death, or their ever having lived. The inevitable outcome of this point of view is to commit suicide. Christening a baby, attending a bar mitzvah, getting married, celebrating a birthday, visiting a graveside, are all rituals which take us under the surface of life—they are psychological means to going deeper, getting to the heart of things. A gravestone is not for the benefit of the dead person. It is an anchorpoint for the minds of the bereaved, to help them affirm that this person really lived. With this knowledge, they can hold that person's value and memory as active forces for health and empowerment as they live their own lives.

The brand of religion one chooses to pursue is not so

important. The differences between religions are only differences of style and technique. Christ, Buddha, Shiva, and Mohammed would have got on just fine. In a sense, any spiritual path will do. To not have some kind of spiritual practice in one's life, however, is a serious mistake. . . .

> I have treated many hundreds of patients. Among those in the second half of life—that is to say over thirty-five—there has not been one whose problem, in the last resort, was not that of finding a religious outlook on life.
>
> —Carl Jung

> A poet's job is not to save the soul of a man, but to make it worth saving.
>
> —James E. Fletcher, quoted in *Wingspan*

FAMILY ISN'T ENOUGH

Many men, if questioned, locate the purpose for their lives in pursuing the well-being of their family. So it might surprise you to learn that this is not enough. Altruistic as it may sound, to make one's family all-important is spiritually parasitic. Living through your wife is very bad for you both. Making your children your purpose for living puts an unbearable burden on them. Raising a family may take up almost your whole life. Yet it isn't the heart of your existence, because one day it will be over. You, and the universe, are the only two concerns that last.

In *Fire in the Belly*, Sam Keen tells of being helped by an older man friend while going through a painful divorce. This man told him, "There are two questions a man must ask himself: The first is, 'Where am I going?' The second is, 'Who will go with me?' If you ever get these questions in the wrong order you are in trouble!" Most of us get the order wrong.

LEARNING FROM THE PAST

"Where am I going?" is the critical question of our lives. "Where have I come from?" might hold some of the answers. We know where we have come from: there is a trail running back behind you through the centuries, all the way to a Cro-Magnon hunter half a million years ago. You are alive and here today because he was wise enough, tough, skillful, nurturing, coura-geous, to be able to form loving relationships, nurture chil-dren, work with the forces of nature, and survive. (And his partner or partners were likewise.) You have the same superb capacities that he did. The problem is how to awaken them.

ECOLOGY AS A SPIRITUAL PATH

We have already said (in the chapter on work) that your ulti-mate job as a man is to preserve life. This doesn't just mean your little corner of life—your kids and your backyard. Living a life that makes ecological sense isn't just a practical challenge but involves an inner change of orientation too. The biologist who goes out to study the rainforest from an objective point of view comes back changed by the experience. The nights under the massive forest canopy and the days peering into nature's mysteries have captured his soul. He changes from a dried-up "nerd" to a passionate and newly balanced man. (Annie Dil-lard's Pulitzer prize-winning book *Pilgrim at Tinker Creek* is a good place to start if you wish to awaken this perception.)

There's every indication that ecology is becoming a new religion, especially for idealistic young people. It's equally pos-sible, though, that the needs of our time will simply transform our existing religions to something more vibrant and pur-poseful, by turning more to nature and wildness and less to dogma and intellectual head-tripping. There are already emerging ecologically aware forms of Christianity and Islam, Hinduism and so forth. Buddhism is already a superbly ecological religion.

Many people are attracted to a more natural life, not just from "save the earth" concerns but because they are pulled to it by the wildness in their own nature. Indeed there are many who would claim not to be religious at all, yet the wilderness and the ocean are already their spiritual homes. Surfers, mountaineers, hikers, are responding to this call. Even an old person growing roses is seeking the spiritual. The thirst for wildness is with us every day. The more artificial life gets, the more people strive to redress the balance. Nature always offers the happiest way for humans. The closer modern man gets to inner and outer wildness, the better things will go.

This takes more than just sitting in a forest! Ancient cultures knew that to "arrive" as a man in harmony with the outer world requires a long journey. It's an involved process requiring effort and care from parents and elders, lasting many years. It's not enough to eat sprouts and be groovy; serious disciplines and processes have to be gone through.

INITIATION—THE BREAKTHROUGH TO MANHOOD

Once when I was a teenager, I was swimming in the ocean, when a beautiful young mother and two children came down to the shore. One of the children threw some stones in the water. "Be careful not to hit that man" cried the mother. I looked about surprised—I hadn't known anyone else was in the water. Then I realized—she meant me! It made my day!

We believe being a man is a matter of size and age alone. The results of this are clear to see—boys in men's bodies, everywhere you look. In centuries gone by, becoming a man was a long, planned process. It required ritual and effort and the deliberate, active intervention of the whole community. This ritual and effort, although very diverse in its forms around the planet, was universally practiced in every society, from Eskimo to Zulu, by every race and at every time. It was the first thing anthropologists noticed when they visited cultures other than their own. It had a name. It was called "initiation."

Kikuyu men, to take just one example, would take the youngsters at a certain age away from the women, and the boys would go without food for three days. Then the older men would arrive, cut their veins to fill a bowl with blood, which the young men drank. Most of shudder to hear this—what is this all about? Perhaps it tells the boys—men can nourish too. The boys are then fed, cared for, prepared for rituals and given intense attention by the older men. In the days that follow, the old men recount the creation myths, stories, and songs that are part of being male in that culture. They charge the boys with responsibilities to the people, and the land. The boys feel their connection beyond just family to all men who have lived in that place, and see themselves as a link in time and space that goes on into the future. Similar activities carry the girls into womanhood, separate and unknown to the boys.

INITIATORY JOURNEYS YOU MIGHT HAVE MADE

Lacking these processes today, we often find ourselves drawn to create such experiences unconsciously. One night, while reading the work of Joseph Campbell, the renowned mythologist, I realized I had made at least one of these journeys myself. I'm sure many men will recognize the pattern from their own youth. According to Campbell, the initiatory journey always has three steps:

1. A separation from home and family and all that is familiar.
2. A frightening, difficult, but exhilarating journey, helped along by unexpected hospitality from strangers

and help from mystical allies. This enables you to face
your vulnerability and break out of many youthful fears
and neuroses.

3. Finally, a return home: the traveler apparently the
same person, but forever changed.

When I was seventeen, I saw a
poster inviting young Australians
to go alone and live in a New
Guinea village and experience
"stone age" life. The scheme was
organized by a student group
wanting to bridge gaps between Papua-New Guinean culture and the West. I joined up and went. With a New
Guinean host, I stayed on the coast of West New Britain,
with people who still wore leaf clothes, lived in grass
houses, and told creation stories around the fires at night-
time. It was scary and I was often way out of my depth, but
it was also a beautiful time. On the journey home, ill with
dysentery, and still culture-shocked, I stayed at a coastal
airstrip with a young Australian man called Marcus, who
was a patrol officer. He was an "older" man of about thirty-
five. Though I didn't know it at the time, Marcus was one of
the people on that trip who represented the "helper" or
"mentor" of the initiatory journey. While I waited for the
floodwaters to recede from the airstrip and a plane to take me
home, I filled in the time talking with him about life. We sat
each night looking out at the Bismarck Sea, listening to the
waves on the black beach sand and the deep-voiced chanting
from fishermen in passing canoes.

One night he told me about his own childhood—on a farm
near Wilsons Promontory in Victoria. How one hot afternoon,
his father had received a telegram informing him that his own
father had died. Marcus watched while his father ate his meal

> Marcus, still just a little
> boy, followed him . . .
> mesmerized

quietly and then set off into the bush at dusk. Marcus, still just a little boy, followed him at a distance, mesmerized.

He found his father sitting on a hilltop, overlooking Corner Inlet, with a harmonica, playing a long and mournful dirge. He had never heard his father play this instrument before. After listening for a time and fearful of being discovered, he left and snuck back home.

In Port Moresby, on the way home, I realized I had no gifts to bring my parents and so I sold my air ticket on the Brisbane-Melbourne sector, to raise funds. Then I bought some artifacts and hitchhiked the last thousand miles home (an adventure in itself). A week later, at about two A.M., I found myself at a highway phone booth on a deserted road about twenty miles from home. I experienced a curious impulse—to not go home at all, but just keep traveling. I solved it uniquely. My tired, hungry, grimy self phoned home, to be rescued by my long-suffering parents! But my inner self has been traveling ever since. Like many of my generation, I'm still on the road.

I'm sure you too have made such journeys. The memory is so ancient and the idea so much part of human development that we may carry it out in part without realizing it. The magic still works.

In older times, these journeys were properly organized. People knew what they were doing. The Native American young men would sit motionless on a mountain top seeking their vision dream. In the forest below stealthy watchers guarded them from pumas and other dangers. The young people of the old cultures were too loved and too valuable to be endangered needlessly.

A friend of mine, who teaches rock climbing to young offenders and business executives, explained to me that in this apparently dangerous activity the safety is total. It isn't through pointless danger that we grow, but through the utmost care and trust in each other. When young men steal cars, or run wild, they are trying to recapture this process, but no mentors are there to guide them.

WHAT ARE THE ELEMENTS OF A GOOD INITIATION?

First there is a clean break with the parents, after which the boy goes to the forest, desert, or wilderness. The second is a wound that the older men give the boy, which could be a scarring of the skin, a cut with a knife, a brushing with nettles, a tooth knocked out.

The old initiators took the boys into the forest or the desert to give them a great prize—to teach them that they themselves were sacred beings. That's what initiation means. There was fear involved, and symbolic wounding, but this was done with great care and for important reasons. It was never done sadistically. The masks, dancing, rituals, magical teaching, and adoption of totems gave the young man a strong sense of belonging and honor.

A Christian missionary in Uganda in the 1970s observed that certain of the young men in his college were thin and unhealthy, they lacked confidence, did not take wives, and lived very poorly. He discovered that these were the ones who through circumstance—illness or travel—had missed out on initiation. Their lives just seemed stalled.

The attention young men received at initiation was simply an intensification of the continuous involvement that uncles, grandfathers, cousins, and older siblings took with boys and young men to convey to them living skills, and male spirit and ways of doing things. None of these cultures would dream of leaving masculine development to chance in the way that we do.

Michael Ventura, in a magnificent essay called "The Age of Endarkenment," speaks of adolescent wildness and its challenge to our lack of ideas. Their music, their fashions, their words, their codes, he says, *announce that the initiatory moment has come.* Those extravagances are a request for a response. Ventura remarks:

> *Tribal people everywhere greeted the onset of puberty, especially in males, with elaborate and excruciating initiations—a practice that wouldn't have been necessary unless their young were as extreme as ours. . . . The tribal adults didn't run from this moment in their children as we do; they celebrated it. They would assault their adolescents with, quite literally, holy terror; rituals that had been kept secret from the young until that moment. . . . rituals that focused upon the young all the light and darkness of the tribe's collective psyche, all its sense of mystery, all its questions and all the stories told to both harbor and answer those questions. . . . The crucial word here is focus. The adults had something to teach, stories, skills, magic, dances, visions, rituals. In fact, if these things were not learned well and completely, the tribe could not survive. . . . Tribal cultures satisfied the craving while supplying the need, and we call that initiation. This practice was so effective that usually by the age of fifteen a tribal youth was able to take his or her place as a fully responsible adult.*

There is more involved than just "hanging out" with the older men. The best of the culture has to be transmitted deliberately by the old men to the young. My school friend who killed himself was a science nut, proud of his atheism. The science of the Sixties was very mechanical—it was all just atoms and molecules, and saw people as little more than rats. This was before the death dance of the Vietnam War stirred up a fertile and life-celebrating counterculture in response. We received no wisdom, no ritual, no charge with a purpose in living, there was no sense of the sacred in our high school lives. In his case, this lack was fatal.

DESIGNING INITIATION TODAY

There are many threshold events in the lives of young people that have aspects of initiation, and could, if we chose, be made more special and helpful in giving them a good start. For boys, owning a car, and/or getting a license, is a significant step. A driver's license means that mobility and participation in the adult world are suddenly possible. A car brings independence and a great boosted sex life! One is also suddenly able to endanger one's own and other people's lives—so there's a massive jump in responsibility, too. A policeman I know took his son to get his driving license, and then drove him to the morgue. He explained gently what he intended to do, and the boy, very nervous, nonetheless consented. The two of them then went and quietly looked at some of the dead bodies stored in the cold room.

The father wanted the boy, without hysteria, but with full solemnity, to know that death was real.

Some families prefer a little less intensity, but it's worth having a meal, and inviting uncles and aunts—i.e. not the young mans friends, but his elders, and celebrating this rite of passage to driverhood.

Other thresholds include the first job; the first date. The final school exams are a major and important mark of maturity (perhaps too important). They, too, merit celebration and support. Puberty markers—like a bar mitzvah—call out for creative celebration and adult support.

Having one's own apartment, surviving away from Mom's apron strings, feeding oneself and paying the rent are important things to experience. Young men who go from Mom to wife without a self-sufficient phase between always lack a certain something, like the uninitiated Ugandan men mentioned earlier. Be sure that your son learns to look after himself, well away from your fridge and washing machine, as early as you can.

THE WOUND

> *Where a man's wound is, that is where his genius will be.*
> —Mircea Eliade

There is an ingredient of initiation that puzzles many people. This is the concept of the wound. Why the need for hurting? The wound has multiple meanings. Boys get wounded anyway—in body and soul, in a hundred different ways. Ritual injury is used to cleanse all preceding injuries and make them heroic instead of tragic. Just as children in a lot of psychic pain will often burn or cut themselves to distract them from the inner pain, the ritual pain erases and makes special the previous experience. I personally believe this is a very dangerous idea, nonetheless. Female mutilation and circumcision of males are rituals that have gone too far, they damage more than they give back. More warlike and violent societies have the harshest initiations. We must search for a middle path that is a courage-proving and memorable experience, not a destructive one.

In attempting to explain why initiation in so many parts of the world involves physical pain, Robert Bly reminds us of the inner process teenage boys are inflicting on themselves:

Everyone knows this tendency of boys to take risks and seek heroism. It makes sense to formalize (and therefore make safer) this craving for physical intensity as a mark of crossing a threshold.

> *Early adolescence is the time traditionally chosen for initiation to begin and we all recall how many injuries we received at that age. Adolescence is the time of risk for boys and that risk-taking is also a yearning for initiation. Something in the adolescent male wants risk, courts danger, goes out to the edge, even to the edge of death.*

Perhaps the best equivalents we have are the well-conducted and intense outdoor experiences such as Outward Bound. The danger is that these may become like summer camp—a commodity you buy for your children, carried out by jaded strangers. Real initiation involves the adults who care about this child, community members who are committing themselves long term to their well-being and welcoming them into the circle of adults. In my book *Raising Boys*, this is explored more fully.

AN INITIATION HE NEEDED LIKE A HOLE IN THE HEAD
(A news item from Associated Press)

A man who was shot through the skull with an arrow by a friend trying to knock a fuel can off his head survived with no brain damage. Surgeons removed the arrow from Mr. Anthony Roberts' head by drilling a larger hole around the tip at the skull's back, and pulling it through. Mr. Roberts was shot on Saturday at the friend's home in Grant's Pass, about 200 miles south of Portland, Oregon. Mr. Roberts, an unemployed carpenter, lost his right eye. At a hospital news conference, Mr. Roberts initially told reporters he was walking though a park, when he heard a bow fired and then felt the arrow hit. Later he told them his friend was trying to knock the gallon can off his head as part of an initiation into a rafting and outdoor group called Mountain Men Anonymous.

Investigators said there was no doubt the can story was true. Mr. Roberts said he was drinking with friends when the accident occurred. "I don't think that's a good initiation," he said. "I think a hug would be better."

If the arrow had been an inch closer to his nose, it would have severed major blood vessels, and Mr. Roberts could have died on the spot. Dr. Delashaw said, "I've never seen anything like it."

"I feel really stupid," Mr. Roberts said.

THE WOUND TURNS TO GOLD

If your life has been full of difficulty and damage, you have only two choices. You can either stay caught in the suffering, a victim for always. Or you can turn the suffering into something special. This involves making a journey through suffering and out the other side.

> *If you want to change the way you are with your sons, and your daughters, then my experience is you need to feel how you were hurt, and how you were wounded.*
> —Marvin Allen in "Wild Man Weekend" documentary

We know that the greatest artists, the really great leaders, did not have cozy suburban lives. They suffered and somehow they "turned this around."

A close friend of mine is a calm, soft spoken professional and a family man. He grew up with a father who was quite the opposite—erratic and moody, prone to outbursts of sudden violence. My friend recalls being about eight years old and his father asking him to come on a trip. The boy was scared, hid behind his mother's skirts and did not want to go. While the father yelled and stormed about the house in a rage, the boy ran to his bedroom and got into bed. Moments later the father burst into the room, lifted the whole bed, and upturned it on top of the boy who was then trapped beneath it on the floor.

When the boy grew up he became a career-driven achiever, yet never felt really happy. Only with the onset of midlife did the pain of these experiences begin to catch up with him. He began experiencing all kinds of alarming physical reactions—panic attacks, sensory distortions—but luckily did not panic or take medication. Through talking over the experiences, he made the link with his childhood and accessed many memories that had been pushed away as too painful. In time, and with help, he became more at ease with himself, able to take better care of himself and emotionally more peaceful and flowing. He also

> The father burst into the room, lifted the whole bed, and upturned it on top of the boy

made major career changes, took a long holiday with his family, and set about a very different rhythm of life based on fulfillment rather than external achievement.

THE EXPERIENCE OF INITIATION

Charles Perkins is one of the best known Australian indigenous men. For a time as Head of the Department of Aboriginal Affairs, a graduate in psychology and anthropology and holder of the Order of Australia, Perkins was the leading figure in Aboriginal politics in the 1980s. In 1990, Perkins did a remarkable thing. He became formally initiated as a man of the Arunta people—the clan into which he was born and from which he was stolen by welfare authorities as a child. It began quite simply, when an elder confronted him, late one night, at a campfire meeting in the desert. The old man gave Perkins a tirade about his life and achievements, ending with the simple statement of fact, "There's another world you don't know properly." Perkins realized the old man was right and that he did not understand the very thing he was fighting for. He was not a real Aboriginal, because he had not undergone the process of becoming one. Perkins accepted the invitation. Here, in his own words, he conveys the effect on him of this experience:

> . . . it is beyond, I think, your imagination. I could never tell anyone, explain what it means; it's just too much and nobody knows but me and the people in the ceremonies

> *what happened and what it all means. It just boggles the mind, it really does.*
>
> *There are two worlds . . .*
>
> *You sit there at night, with the fires burning and maybe 200 people dancing, it was awe inspiring . . . you're going back 50,000 years in time. It writes new chapters in your brain.*

It was not just a personal transformation. Perkins believed that this way held the key to the rehabilitation of Aboriginal people, away from spiraling poverty, drunkenness, and violence. Of his life before initiation, he was quoted as saying he often felt he was watching life, rather than living it:

> *Unless you drink the water or suck a few leaves, or kick a stone or smell the flowers, you might as well be living in a movie.*

When I went through the ceremonies, the world changed. The trees were different, the leaves were different, the grass was different, the hills were different, the air was different. I am looking at a tree and one day it is a tree and the next day it was my friend. I saw somebody else there. I was at home.

MEETING THE WILD MAN

One way to understand the meaning of initiation is to say that it is "a journey to meet the Wild Man." The Wild Man is not easy to explain, although most men can in some way relate to the concept. The wild man is not savage, or violent, but he is spontaneous, and intuitive. He is the source of creative brilliance. He is what happens when we let go of control, and trust to something inside us to do the right thing. The Wild

Man teaches that we don't have to pretend to be good, but that we have power and integrity latent inside us, if we trust it. Abandoning yourself to wildness turns out to be the most harmonious and generative thing you can do. (Fans of Taoism and Lao Tsu will feel right at home here.) When we are good, we are okay, but when we are "wild" we are geniuses. Any man who makes or builds things, who creates a garden, who plays a musical instrument, who has ever been a lover, knows that you are better when you "let go" and follow your impulses.

Our love of trees, the outback, waves and water, animals, growing things, music, children and women, all stem from our wild nature. The most creative men are close to the Wild Man and borrow his power.

All masculine confidence, of the inner kind, arises in the domain of the Wild Man. Also, the way to develop male spirituality is to "know" the Wild Man—to converse with him, not to become him. Jesus, Mohammed, and Buddha were well at ease with the Wild Man, spending time in the wilderness, using nature as their place of prayer and reflection. All bore his hallmarks—being unpredictable and nonconformist with the established order of their times, yet at the same time disciplined and true to their inner voices.

In her wonderful book, *Women Who Run with the Wolves*, C. P. Estes recommends precisely the same to women—that they need a civilized part and a wild intuitive part, in balance. The over-civility of women—excessive niceness—endangers them, just as much as it does men.

We have to learn to trust that our original nature, our inner self, is good. To be convinced of this you have only to look closely at a baby. Clearly we are all born beautiful. This is why birth is so moving. Wordsworth was right—we come to earth "trailing clouds of glory." Through initiation, we get hooked up to the grid of our inborn wisdom—that knows how to breathe, how to sing, how to recognize lies, how to be brave.

We have just lived through an era when women were given the power to tell us how to be men. To be macho in any manner has become unfashionable. And yet, every man has a strong streak of macho in his DNA. To deny it and suppress it can be deadly to men (and to the culture). Such denial can leave us depressed, without energy or passion or identity. The concept was addressed in the hugely popular and hugely misunderstood book *Iron John* by Robert Bly.

Asa Baber, the provocative masculinist writer, explains what Bly was about.

What Bly is proposing is that every modern male, has lying at the bottom of his psyche, a large primitive man covered with hair down to his feet. Making contact with this wild man is the process that still hasn't taken place in contemporary culture. Freud, Jung, and Wilhelm Reich are three men who had the courage to go down into the pond and accept what's there. The job of modern males is to follow them down.

Accepting what is dark down there—what he calls "the shadow"—is another task that Bly assigns to any man who would discover his true male self and become an initiated male. Under Bly's urging, men are beginning to explore this shadow side of their personalities. Anger, aggression, grief, feelings of abandonment and rejection, rage, confusion—all the varied dark and shadowy forces that whirl around like demons in the male psyche—these are things we have tried to deny or ignore in order to be acceptable and admired.

But we have tried much too hard to be nice and we have essentially handed over the job of self-definition to others. This turns out to have been self-destructive. We emasculate and feminize ourselves to gain female approval and then we hope against all available evidence that our masculine energies will leave us alone. But is that likely?

Face it: For most men, the hope that our energy will fade away is in vain. Witness the fact that our sexuality emerges at a very early age—and carries with it a beautiful immediacy, from spontaneous erections to wet dreams and vivid fantasies. This immediacy of male sexuality lasts well into our adulthood, even into old age for many men. Are we really going to be able to suppress all of that energy? And why should we repudiate such a unique and wonderful drive?

To use a Bly analogy, "The Widow Douglas wanted Huck Finn to be nice. And after he has floated down the river with the black man, Aunt Sally wants to adopt him and 'civilize' him. Huck says, 'I can't stand it. I been there before.'" Sounds familiar, doesn't it.

The wildman lives in every man. He is beautiful and divine. He has enormous fundamental energy and a great love for the world. He is just as much a nurturer and protector and creator as any female figure, but he will do that nurturing and protecting in his own masculine way. It is time for the Wild Man in us to be celebrated without shame. That celebration is part of what our revolution is about. It is our job as men to know ourselves better so that we can contribute more to this world and be more honest with ourselves. We have a right to our revolution, in other words. An absolute right.

—Asa Baber in *Wingspan*

VENUS BAY—EDGE OF THE WILD

If you are a man, too much civilization will kill you

Mine was a close-knit family, in that deathly English kind of way, and as immigrants to Australia, we became even more isolated. My sister and I were on the edge of explosive adolescence, and the family was turning into a pressure cooker. Everyone looked forward to camping trips away from home, and just wondered if we had to take each other along!

The day dawned sunny and perfectly still. We had the place to ourselves and walked by the water's edge, just taking it all in. The Australian coastline still has places where the forest runs down to the sea and a sense of wild nature pervades. After we had gone a mile or so along the sea edge, I decided to go for a swim and walked into the trees behind the dunes for a private place to change into my swimming shorts. Standing with my clothes off, in a glade of sunlight among twisted tea-tree and vines, I was aware of a combination—my body unfamiliarly naked, warm sunlight on my pale skin and the aroma of honeysuckle. Half-lit glades festooned with creepers lay all around. There was a sense of total, primal wildness that was seductive, welcoming, and mysterious all at the same time. Sexuality was in there along with other more global feelings. At that moment I simply felt more alive than I had ever recalled feeling in my whole life. I could have run off into that forest and never returned.

This feeling of profound connection is every child's birthright. We should be able to build our life around it. All art, music, religion, poetry, is an attempt to return to it. It is at the heart of what we seek in lovemaking. Yet it is the very opposite of what we build around ourselves in the modern world.

Robert Bly puts it very bluntly: "If you are a man," he says, "civilization will kill you." American Indian people shared the same reaction when they saw with horror the white man's cities and towns. The Amazon people say it today. They don't so much fear the white man's world, rather they are horrified by its toxicity to a man's soul. They look at our world and pity us.

THE TIME OF ASHES

We are given a blueprint, of sorts, for the shape of a man's life. Adolescence is allowed to be rocky. Then you settle down. You work and raise kids. Then you retire and die. Nothing too alarming about that. But it never goes according to plan. A huge and important stage which you are never told about lies in wait. It looks like bad news and it's the complete opposite. It's the time of Ashes.

The late thirties and early forties seem to be the time that this often happens. Usually around this time of life, something goes badly wrong. Perhaps a baby is stillborn. Or your wife stops loving you. Your father, sturdy and seemingly immortal, gets cancer and dies before your eyes. You develop health problems yourself. A car accident smashes up your body. Your career tumbles down like a pack of cards. Suddenly there is shame, error, and grief all around you. Welcome to the Ashes.

The trigger for my journey downwards was a miscarriage—an abrupt end to a much-wanted pregnancy. When my partner felt the contractions after only three months of pregnancy, I swung into auto-pilot. I drove us to the hospital calmly and safely. I remember standing with her, soaking in the shower room at the hospital, catching in my wet hands small pieces of our hoped-for child. Still seemingly unaffected, I conducted a two-day seminar straight after the event. Then the impact came. I sank slowly into a black hole that lasted for over a year. My trademark optimism and confidence evaporated in the face of powerless grief. I became unlovable, self-absorbed, barely wanting to get out of bed. My moods served only to push away my partner, who was handling her own grief on her own timetable. I drifted toward non-being.

Somehow, gradually, as time went on, I softened inside. I was so confused, and on unfamiliar ground, which meant a good thing started to happen. I had to swallow my pride and let friends help me—which for me was not easy. Gradually, over time, I rebuilt a sense of self that incorporated a new understanding. What I now know is that I am like everyone else—totally weak, totally vulnerable, lucky that life tests my limits so rarely, lucky just to be alive. In a word, humbled. I now knew how bad other people could feel, and could have the beginnings of compassion.

You do not have to experience total devastation in order to grow into a mature man, but you have to know its possibility deep in your bones—to discover that you are not all-powerful and your dreams may well not come true. Thus you make the journey down into Ashes. If you get the message, you move on, but if you don't really go to the bottom, then it might have to all happen again. Finally you get the message and only then do you go from being a careless boy to a more open-hearted and compassionate man.

HEALING THROUGH HEALTHY SHAME

An old man and a younger man are on a long camping trip across the desert. For the first few days the young man is somewhat tense and quiet. The older man notices this but just lets it be. Finally the younger man begins to talk. He is the manager of a fruit-growing property, and in the winter, just a few months ago, backed a trailer over his own three-year-old son. Disaster was narrowly avoided—the ground was muddy and wet, and the boy was pressed down into the mud. Miraculously, he was only bruised and shocked.

The young man had been distraught for weeks. Close friends and family told him not to worry, it could have happened to anyone. He recovered somewhat, but he could not put the incident out of his mind. Even on this trip, a much-needed break, he was still experiencing flashbacks and cold sweats. The old man was silent. He did not reassure or minimize the feelings of the young man, who sat also silent, feeling the familiar knotting in his gut as he once again relived the experience.

"Exactly what did people say to you?" the older man asked eventually.

"They said it was an accident. Not to blame myself. It could happen to anyone. That kind of thing. "

"Hmmm." The old man was quiet again for a while.

"They're wrong then," he said all of a sudden, jolting the young man from his thoughts.

"Wh-what do you mean?" he asked.

"It was a really stupid thing to do," said the old man with almost infinite gentleness in his voice. "You're lucky your young fella wasn't killed."

The young man was suddenly glad it was dark around their small campfire. His face flushed and hot tears began to run down his cheeks.

"I thought my wife was looking after him. We'd just had a fight. I started the tractor. I never looked. I was thinking, it's her bloody job to keep the kids inside, and I never looked."

By now the older man was alongside the younger one, gripping his shoulder with one hand. The young man simply pitched forward onto the sand, wailing out loud. The older man moved alongside him and put one hand on his arm. The young man seemed to continue his curving fall into the old man's chest, holding on and sobbing great, gulping sobs. After a time the sobbing stopped. He became aware of the warmth of the older man's shirt against his cheek, sat up a little, and looked at the starry desert sky over his shoulder. A deep calmness settled into him; calmer than he had ever felt.

THE GRIEF THAT MAKES US WHOLE

Every man needs an Ashes time in his life. To discover that, in spite of all optimism and effort, one is still vulnerable. To fall into despair at these times, though very inviting, is to miss the point. Grief is cleansing, despair is just standing still. The key is to let your feelings out.

Life is about going on, being active, making decisions, taking steps, not knowing how it will work out. Life is a tough business. If a man is able at these times to allow himself to cry and share some of his pain with his friends, then he comes through a better man. He no longer looks disdainfully at poor, handicapped, or weak people. He realizes they are just like him. His capacity for compassion deepens enormously. The Ashes time completes what has begun in adolescence—the making of a real man.

IN A NUTSHELL

• Think about where you are going. What you will do when your children are gone, and your wife is dead? What is your life about—when there is just you?

• Create a space for yourself that is separate, so you can get to know yourself apart from your roles.

• Realize that for men, nature is where your home is. Spend time there. Pursue wildness—especially if you live in the city. Take deliberate action—like walking on the beach—so that you can re-attune yourself to the rhythms of earth, ocean, and sky.

• Be religious. Especially favor religions that dance, bang drums, sing, or sit in total silence.

• Take a year off when you turn forty, and do things you have postponed, or always wanted to do. Re-evaluate whether you wish to continue in the way you have been going, or make changes.

• Each year, around the time of your birthday, spend three days in complete solitude. Think about whether you need some kind of initiation into manhood—to move from being a perpetual adolescent.

• Learn about the ancient culture of the land you live on. The Native American culture, mood, and temperament will be very instructive.

• Accept times of great misfortune—a marriage breakdown, sickness, or business failure—as essential steps to getting free. Roll in the Ashes. Don't be afraid of pain, grief, sadness, weakness, or failure. They enrich your humanness.

• Go looking for the Wild Man.

12 **Men's Groups**

I HOPE THAT reading this book has given you some good ideas for your own life, which you may have already begun to implement. But perhaps you are feeling a little overwhelmed. One problem with the whole "self-help" and "self-improvement" scene is the expectation that we can change things all on our own. Contemporary man has been plagued by this illusion. When this solitary approach fails, we conclude that nothing can be changed after all, and give up. So today, many young men are brashly overconfident, and most older men are depressed!

Since writing the first edition of *The Secret Life of Men* (published in Australia as *Manhood*), I have learned more about the importance of having a male community. To make personal change easier, and to make global change possible, we have to build and belong to a community of men who are working toward similar goals. Small groups of men who are willing to meet regularly and talk can give each other huge insights, enormous amounts of encouragement, and occasional kicks in the butt—all essential to keeping you open and moving toward liberation! If you want your life as a man to really get moving, then you should consider joining or starting a men's group. Here are some guidelines, if you are interested.

HOW MEN'S GROUPS WORK

In a living room not far from where you are reading this,

odds are that a group of eight or nine men meets every couple of weeks to talk about their lives. Their wives or partners are happy to vacate the house on that night because they like the results—a happier, more balanced, stronger, and more peaceful man.

There are thousands of men's groups in the U.S. Therapist-turned-activist Guy Corneau has single-handedly founded three hundred groups in Canada. In the UK, Germany, South America, and New Zealand, men's groups are forming, writing newsletters, "Internetting," holding conferences, and getting excited. Different emphases are emerging: in the U.S. there are special efforts being made to bridge men of different races. In Australia good links are being forged with Aboriginal people, and there is a focus on the mentoring of adolescent boys. In Northern Ireland there is an emphasis on helping young fathers to do a better job.

The structure of a men's group is based on some key guidelines. There is no pressure to speak unless you wish to. There is an emphasis on hearing someone out, rather than interrupting with argument or well-meaning advice. (Most people get plenty of this in their normal lives.) The emphasis is also on speaking from the heart, not "discussing" or "theorizing."

Men's groups can be emotional at times. Something very freeing happens when a private space is set aside, when the rules are "no bullshitting," and "say what you feel." If men know their stories will be heard and honored, then a great deal finds its way to the surface.

Men's groups are also very practical. The chosen topic of the night may be "how to discipline your kids," or "how to break out of an alienating career and make time to live." It might be some frank discussion about sex, or it might be more crisis-driven—shoring up a man wounded from marital combat, or a man whose wife has just that week been diagnosed with cancer. I've listened in men's groups to older men talk about war trauma, honestly, for the first time after decades of silent suffering.

Young men find surrogate fathers and uncles in the group. Depressed older men find a reason to feel they have something to offer. The ethics of men's groups are strong—particularly about never acting (or even speaking) violently to women, children, or each other. Men's group talk has a style that is very different from women's talk—there's less tiptoeing, and less tendency to agree with everything you say.

Men's groups usually meet in homes, though occasionally they are church-based or meet in a health center. Most are general purpose, some are specifically for men with violence problems or health or marital concerns. A group may close its membership once it is running, though some will invite new members periodically. The most common way to start is to invite a few friends and begin your own. Some groups use a book (such as this one) as a discussion starter or generate a list of topics agreed by members. Leadership tends to be rotated, rather than having no leader at all—acknowledging that men like structure and are goal-oriented.

Men's groups usually have rules (no put-downs, confidentiality) and there is a tendency to confront bullshit or irresponsibility. "You're neglecting your goddamn kids, man! When are you going to wake up to yourself!" "Well, sure you could leave your wife, but you'd be an idiot to do it. Why don't you talk to her and tell her what you're feeling?" "You're tired, buddy. You and your wife need a vacation." And so on. You don't have to "spill your guts" in a men's group—there isn't any pressure. Perhaps for that very reason, though, you soon find yourself sharing your life, prompted by the similarities of your own experiences with those being shared by the other men. You get practical tips for living and feel you can breathe more deeply, all at the same time! It adds a sense of relaxation to your life (very different from getting drunk or going fishing) because the changes are cumulative. Your life starts to make more sense.

Most men's groups reach a point where they organize to get away for weekends. In groups where most men are fathers, activities are often planned to include the youngsters. Some groups exist specifically for dads and daughters, or dads and sons, to spend time together supported by some resources and structure.

Men's groups can become activist in nature, as a counterbalance to all the talk. Fred Hollows, a famous Australian eye-surgeon who took his skills to the third world, belonged to such a group. When a row of tobacco billboards were erected along his favorite stretch of coast, he went with his friends and chainsawed them down on a dark and windy night. The company replaced them with steel posts some months later. Fred's men's group returned with steel cutting equipment and did it again. After that the company gave up.

WHERE THIS MAY LEAD

What about the big picture? Men's needs require changes in legislation and the workplace. Paternity leave, flexible working hours. As men wean off the earn and spend cycle, the economy and the wider world will be affected in many ways. People will consider other necessary changes: the way that boys are treated in schools; the access situation for fathers; exploitation of young men in sport; sexual abuse of boys; men in the military; rape in prisons; the right of children to have and know their fathers; and the prevention of rape and harassment of women. The field is wide.

MAKING A WORLD THAT IS KINDER TO MEN, WILL MAKE MEN KINDER

This is the missing piece of the social reform jigsaw. Who knows where it might take us? If you're a man, you're part of it and your actions will make a difference. If you're a woman reading this, thank you for your love and understanding.

IN A NUTSHELL

• The "self-made man" is a myth—we all need the help of others to make and sustain change.

• Join a men's group, or start one with friends.

• Groups that succeed usually have a structure or program, and rotate leadership to keep direction and purpose.

• A planet-wide movement for men's liberation and betterment is gathering momentum. And about time!

FUTURE DREAMING

Men in the future will . . .

Work less, play more. Earn less, spend less. Parent more, stay married longer. Live longer. Be safer to be around.

They will also . . .

Have more friends, and be closer to those friends.
Watch less sport and play more sport.
Take a long-term interest in outdoor and wilderness pursuits, of a quieter and more experiential kind.
Become almost religious about, quietly dedicated to, ecological activism.

As lovers they will . . .

Be better in bed, more alive in their bodies, but also more confident, less needy, more friendly—in less of a hurry.

As fathers men will . . .

Be involved and positive, and willing to take a firm stand, without being carping or intimidating.

As consumers they will . . .

Dress more warmly and colorfully. Wear handmade and decorative but distinctively masculine clothes and artifacts. (The suit and tie will disappear. Like the top hat and the frock coat, they will become historical oddities.)

Drive old but classy cars, and look after them.

Learn to play more musical instruments.

Prefer "world" music and move away from youth-oriented styles or products. The cult of youth will disappear, and young people will be seen as they are, lovely but immature, and certainly not to be envied.

Old age and experience will swiftly be revalued in everything from fashion and movies to employment trends and leadership choices.

Role-models will be people in their fifties and older, especially men and women of a warm and unhurried kind, yet still prickly and confronting, authoritative and humorous.

Existing religions will be revitalized as men take a greater interest in their inner world; and, in addition, new hybrids and forms of ceremony will be evolved—especially those helping men to heal their pasts and to initiate their teenage sons. A gradual blurring of religion and ecology will begin to emerge as a power in its own right.

Many men will, as a kind of ritual choice, take their fortieth year off from work and pursue other goals.

They will then decide whether to continue in their career or make changes.

Most men will also spend a few days each year, around the time of their birthdays, in complete solitude.

Locally organized and well trained groups of men will confront and work with child-abusers, rapists, and wife-beaters, in caring but extremely tough monitoring networks and self-help groups. This will save police resources for more white-collar crime work!

Men will organize themselves and work alongside women in the community, developing vastly different political and activist organizations, tackling local and global issues, using a myriad of computer networks, faxes, and newsletters.

They will alter the face of schools, rewrite the whole nature of childhood, wrest local councils back from business interests, demolish traditional political parties, and work and network with developing countries and native people to learn from them more about how to live, love and heal on this planet.

In a sense, you won't have to choose whether to "join" the Men's Movement, because it includes all men.

It will be as natural as breathing.

ACKNOWLEDGMENTS

George Biddulph, my father, whose sense of adventure brought us to Australia.

My high school teachers, especially Ellen Bicknell, Arthur John, and Brian Caldwell, and all teachers who know the value of praise and going beyond the syllabus.

Tim Haas, John Morris, and Graham Perkin, early mentors who believed in me when I wasn't so sure.

Robin Maslen, who always shares what he knows.

Dr. Colin McKenzie, for giving me a professional start.

Thakur Balak Bramachiri, in Calcutta, who embodied fathering as community action.

My friends including Geoff Best and all the Supervision and Practitioner Groups at the Collinsvale Centre. The Tas CISD team. The Taylor family. Neil Shillito and Simon McCulloch. Wes Carter, Peter Vogel, and everyone in Men's Health and Wellbeing.

Rex Finch, of Finch Publishing, for all his patience, idealism, and hard work.

Laurie Goldsworthy for the eagle image; and everyone in the Green Movement worldwide.

Dave Hancock for his earthy and beautiful photos, and for his encouragement.

Dr. Rex Stoessiger, and Elizabeth Shannon, both of the University of Tasmania.

Paul Whyte for specific help with understanding boys. Alastair Spate for his great writing about play fighting.

Bettina Arndt for helping with the book, and for being a feminist who also cares about men.

All the people who organize our seminars, especially Judi Taylor, and The Playgroup Association, Parent Network UK, Parents Advice Centres Northern Ireland, and Beust Verlag Germany.

Sue McCloskey at Avalon for the careful editing and the chance to improve. And Matthew Lore for bringing our books to America.

And—best till last—to Shaaron and our children, for so much shared and learnt.

PERMISSIONS

Grateful acknowledgement is made to the following people and organizations for permission to include their material in this book. All quoted matter by Robert Bly in this book, unless otherwise stated, is taken from his book, *Iron John*. This material is reproduced with the kind permission of the publishers, Element Books of Shaftesbury, Dorset, UK.

"Male Bashing" which first appeared in *To Be a Man*, K. Thompson (editor) is reproduced with the kind permission of the author, Fredric Hayward, MR Inc., PO Box 163180, Sacramento, California, 95816.

The cartoon, "Trouble at the I'm OK, You're OK Corral," is reprinted with kind permission of The Cartoonist Limited, London. The cartoon, "The Demon," is reprinted from *A Bunch of Poesy*, by Michael Leunig, with the kind permission of Collins/Angus & Robertson Publishers, a division of HarperCollins Publishers Australia.

Sources for brief quotations are given in the bibliography. Where other quotations have been used, every reasonable effort has been made to seek permission and include full accreditation of the source prior to publication.

BIBLIOGRAPHY

Books quoted in the text

Blankenhorn, David. *Fatherless America*, New York: Basic Books, 1995.

Bly, Robert. Iron John. *A Book about Men*, London: Element, 1991.

Dalbey, Gorden. *Healing the Masculine Soul*, Melbourne: Word, 1989.

Elium, Don and Jeanne. *Raising a Son*, California: Beyond Words, 1992.

Embling, John. *Fragmented Lives: A Darker Side of Australian Life*, Melbourne: Penguin, 1986.

Galbraith, J.K. *The Affluent Society*, New York: Penguin, 1999.

Goldberg, Herb. *The New Male*, New York: Bantam, 1984.

Hagan, Kay Leigh (editor). *Women Respond to the Men's Movement*, San Francisco: Pandora/HarperCollins, 1993.

Harding, Christopher (editor). *Wingspan—Inside the Men's Movement*, New York: St. Martins Press, 1992.

Jones, Caroline. *The Search for Meaning* (3), Sydney: ABC/Collins Dove, 1992.

Keen, Sam. *Fire in the Belly*, New York: Bantam, 1992.

Lee, John. *At My Father's Wedding*, New York: Bantam,1991.

Mailer, Norman. *The Prisoner of Sex*, New York: Penguin, 1985.

Miedzian, Myriam. *Boys Will Be Boys*, London: Virago, 1992.

Rhodes, Richard. *Making Love*, New York: Simon & Schuster, 1992.

Rigby, Ken. *Bullying in Schools (and What to Do About It)*, Sydney: ACER Books, 1996.

Schumacher, E.F. *Small is Beautiful*, London: Vintage, 1993.

Skinner, Robin and Cleese, John. *Families and How to Survive Them*, London: Vermilion, 1993.

Thompson, Keith (editor). *To Be a Man: In Search of the Deep Masculine*, Los Angeles: Jeremy Tarcher, 1991.

Articles quoted in the text

Allen, Marvin from the documentary "Wild Man Weekend," SBS Television.

Associated Press "An initiation he needed like a hole in the head," *The Mercury.*

Baldwin, James quoted in *To Be a Man* (Keith Thompson).

Bliss, Sheperd cited in *Wingspan* (Keith Thompson).

Bly, Robert *Bloomsbury Review,* January, 1991.

Camus, Albert quoted in *To Be a Man* (Keith Thompson).

Cooney, Barry "Touching the Masculine Soul," in *Wingspan* (Christopher Harding).

Feinlein, Prof. Walker p.comm. over counter-lunch at the Black Buffalo Hotel, North Hobart.

Follet, Ken from *Night Over Water,* quoted by Barry Oakley, the *Australian Magazine.*

Friedan, Betty "The Second Stage," 1981, cited in *Wingspan* (Christopher Harding).

Gillette, Douglas "Men and Intimacy," in *Wingspan* (Christopher Harding).

Harding, Chris "Men's Secret Societies, 1890s–1990s," in *Wingspan* (Christopher Harding).

Hayward, Frederic "Male Bashing," originally appeared in *To Be a Man* (Keith Thompson).

Kabir quoted in *Iron John* (Robert Bly).

Lawrence, D. H. *Women in Love,* quoted by Barry Oakley in the *Australian Magazine.*

Lawrence, D. H. "Healing," from *The Complete Poems of D. H. Lawrence* quoted in Iron John (Robert Bly).

Leunig, Michael "The Demon," from *A Bunch of Poesy,* Angus & Robertson/HarperCollins, Sydney, 1992.

Leunig, Michael interviewed by Caroline Jones in *The Search for Meaning* (3).

Masters, Robert "Ditching the Bewitching Myth," in *To Be a Man,* (Keith Thompson).

Noa, Jai "The Cripple and the Man," in Baumli, F., (editor) *Men Freeing Men*, New Atlantis Press, 1985.

Simenon, Georges quoted in *Wingspan* (Christopher Harding).

Taylor, George "Longing for the Great Father," in *Wingspan* (Christopher Harding).

Ventura, Michael "Shadowdancing," quoted in *Wingspan* (Christopher Harding).

Videos

Allen, Marvin "Wild Man Weekend," SBS Television.

Bly, Robert (with Bill Moyers), "A Gathering of Men," PBS Television.

ABOUT THE AUTHOR

STEVE BIDDULPH is one of the world's top-selling psychology authors outside the United States. Over three million people in twenty-three languages currently use his books to help raise their kids and regain control of their lives. Steve lectures worldwide using a unique brand of humor, disarming honesty, and directness about the death of love in a consumption-driven world. His books, including *The Secret of Happy Children* and *Raising Boys*, have impacted the discussion about children, community, and human values in much of the world, been debated in the UK parliament, altered government policies in Australia and New Zealand, and finally are available in the U.S.